D0396416

Neal A. Maxwell

WHEREFORE, YE MUST PRESS FORWARD

Deseret Book Company
Salt Lake City, Utah
1977

© 1977 by Deseret Book Company
All rights reserved
Printed in the United States of America

Library of Congress Cataloging in Publication Data

Maxwell, Neal A
    Wherefore, ye must press forward.

    Includes index.
    1. Christian life—Mormon authors.   I.   Title.
BX8656.M39   248′.48′933   77-18066
ISBN 0-87747-685-3

To President Spencer W. Kimball, who, more than anyone I have ever known, epitomizes pressing forward with the skills, strengths, and sweetness that are interwoven in Nephi's prescription, "Wherefore, ye must press forward with a steadfastness in Christ, having a perfect brightness of hope, and a love of God and of all men." (2 Nephi 31:20.) His combination of pressing, hoping, loving, studying, and enduring is an inspiration to us all. His charming modesty, quiet selflessness, and pervasive righteousness are insistent reminders about how we must do likewise.

CONTENTS

ACKNOWLEDGMENTS AND APPRECIATION

To friends who are kind enough to encourage my further efforts at writing, such as William James Mortimer, Ray Haeckel, Jeananne Gruwell, and Lee Ence.

To a family willing, again, to forgo some July evenings that might have been theirs.

Especially to friends like Daniel H. Ludlow, Elizabeth Haglund, Gary Gillespie, Lowell M. Durham, Jr., and Eleanor Knowles, who have brushed and combed the manuscript.

INTRODUCTION

Whether one is newly baptized, reactivated, or already about his Father's business, he faces two challenges: remaining true to the decisions and covenants that have brought him thus far into serious discipleship, and then, both progressing and enduring in his discipleship.

The overwhelming joy of conversion or a new calling is often followed by feelings of being overwhelmed with duties and doctrines. The first joyous feelings are real and give one much-needed initial momentum. But the genuine exhilaration is soon followed by the need to perspire and to pedal.

The straight and narrow way stretches before us. It is no easy escalator; it is not even a gentle slope upward. There are no turnoffs and few scenic views or pauses for one to catch his breath. Saints and prospective Saints are like a moving spectrum along the straight and narrow path of progress. Our different degrees of spiritual development are obvious and should arouse within us neither competitiveness (except that with our former self) nor persistent discouragement.

In such circumstances the wise words of Nephi are addressed to those of us who, whether recently or continuingly, are "in this straight and narrow path which leads to eternal life." We have happily entered in by the first gate. We have the joy and satisfaction of having thus "done according to the commandments," and we have "received the Holy Ghost." (2 Nephi 31:18.)

It is then, however, that Nephi asks: "And now, my beloved brethren, after ye have gotten into this straight and narrow path, I would ask if all is done? Behold, I say unto you, Nay. . . . Wherefore, ye must press forward with a steadfastness in Christ, having a perfect brightness of hope, and a love of God and of all men. Wherefore, if ye shall press forward, feasting upon the word of Christ, and endure to the end, behold, thus saith the Father: Ye shall have eternal life." (2 Nephi 31:19-20.)

Nephi further underscores the importance of what he has said, lest we think there is an easier and alternate route: "And now, behold, my beloved brethren, this is the way; and there is none other way. . . ." (2 Nephi 31:21.) Nephi seems to sense that some of us would, after we "have entered in by the way," "ponder these things in [our] hearts." (2 Nephi 32:1.) He reminds us that the gift of the Holy Ghost will be the means by which we can be shown "all things what [we] should do." (2 Nephi 32:3.)

Nephi does not suggest it will all be a snap, and he speaks in plainness so that we will not misunderstand. He bemoans the fact that given, as you and I have been, great and plain truths about life and salvation, even so, some of us "will not search knowledge, nor understand great knowledge." (2 Nephi 32:7.)

Can one be in the midst of great knowledge and be insensitive to its implications, leaving it unsearched and unappreciated? Quite as easily as some can be in the midst of beauty which they leave unsavored.

This volume addresses itself, therefore, to the challenges that are bound up in pressing "forward with a steadfastness in Christ." The several criteria that Nephi gave can and must take on specific meaning in our lives lest, just as some ask if all is done, others (with perhaps a trace of disappointment) ask, "Is this it?"

Our new (or continuing) performance of discipleship must be carried out in a manner so that the Father can consecrate our performance unto us and so that our performance may be for the welfare of our soul. (See 2 Nephi 32:9.) Proper performances will bring the needed reinforcing joys and satisfactions as we move along the path.

A second and final gate awaits us at the end of the straight and narrow path. We need to press forward in order to reach that ultimate gate beyond which there is ultimate joy. Meanwhile, the straight and narrow path is the only path that can take us there!

Chapter One

ON LETTING GO OF THE WORLD

And Jesus said unto him,
No man, having put his hand
to the plough, and looking back,
is fit for the kingdom of God.
(Luke 9:62.)
The Old Man of the Earth stooped
over the floor of the cave, raised a huge stone,
and left it leaning. It disclosed
a great hole that went plumb down.
"That is the way," he said.
"But there are no stairs." "You must throw
yourself in. There is no other way."
(George MacDonald, *An Anthology*
[London: Geoffrey Bles, 1970], p. 104.)

When we speak of letting go of the world, this does not mean forgoing its sunsets, its beautiful music, nor, best of all, its people. The "world" is a way of life that takes us away from, not toward, God. Away from, not toward, happiness. Away from sense to nonsense.

The Lord's way takes us away from coarseness and crudity, toward civility and gentleness; from carnality, toward a craving for spirituality. There is *nothing* worldly that is really worth holding on to.

Why then is it so hard to give up worldly things? Because we do not see or really deal with the consequences of the two distinct ways of life. However, there is help coming, for the contrasts in the two ways of life are becoming much more stark in our time. The irrepressible issues are surfacing one by one and are confronting us boldly. For all who will see, the reasons for letting go of the world will become ever more clear.

1

Much of the enslavement of evil is proceeding currently under the fashionable banner of liberation. Herr Goebbels, Hitler's minister of propaganda, could never have pulled off what he called the "Big Lie" (the more preposterous, the more believable) on anything like the grand scale that is under way now. The "Big Lie" is in flower, spawned and spread by the father of lies, Lucifer. He who did not care a whit for our agency in the beginning now comes to man in the name of freedom. Milking the legitimate aspirations and yearnings for freedom, exploiting the many injustices that need correction, Lucifer plays siren songs upon the harpstrings of our humanity.

Discipleship has always required that we let go of the world, but to temporize now will simply be more immediately fatal. By letting go of the world, we gain the grasp of an outstretched hand that belongs to Him who was once offered the world; Satan now tries to persuade us through his blandishments that what he offered Jesus (and was turned down) is still a bargain. We, too, must spurn Satan, that loser who knows nothing of real success and who wants to mutualize his misery.

Two alternatives are arrayed before us. We see on one side amorality, anarchy, insensate individuality, abortions, violence, and corruption, and on the other side, liberty, love, sensitivity, respect for life, peace, and integrity. When we know what we know about the alternatives, why do we so often choose as we choose? One reason is that today's disciples live in a time of many terrible trends which, bit by bit, can entangle us like Gulliver.

The webbing of the world contains so many ways to clasp us. The peer pressure that advances one his first step toward the tragedy of alcoholism. The devilish juvenile dare that draws one into fornication, which unrepented of foreshadows later adultery. The cutting of a corner to avoid embarrassment that leads one to lying on an as-needed basis. The natural desire for recognition that is twisted just enough to set a soaring ego free, causing a little leapfrogging of one's perceived competitors

2

and ending up in a hellish heedlessness of others. A tendency to hold back on the giving of one's time and talents that mushrooms into a monastic or hedonistic life-style. A discerning eye for flaws in others that soon focuses on searching for their shortcomings. Little trends later become terrible traits.

Worse still, a hardened justification then sets in that resists introspection. People become good at being bad. Style is praised without regard to substance. Expressions of exclamation ("That's really living!") ignore the dying that is underway.

Significantly, the gospel tells us that we have all sinned and fallen short of the glory of God. It is no use deriving relative comfort from super sinners: the Brinks robbery does not absolve or even obscure the occasional shoplifter's need to set things right with God and man; a dictator's cruelty still leaves a husband's curtnesss to be overcome; and a government's abuse of its borrowing powers does not excuse the expense account that has been padded.

Those of us who have received the law of the gospel are irrevocably accountable for the light and knowledge we have received. Societal trends do not excuse any trends in ourselves.

Trends do not change truths. Unnatural sex is still wrong and self-destructive even if many people come to prefer it, just as the slaughter of Jews was still terribly wrong even though it became commonplace in Europe over a quarter of a century ago. Such trends do not a truth but a tragedy make. Just because something becomes acceptable to man does not make it acceptable to God. In Sodom, and in some respects in today's world, man's norms are but abnormalities in democratic disguise. But such trends are a clear and present danger to serious discipleship, hence the need to press forward.

Baptism by full immersion is best followed by full immersion in the new way of life. Disengagement from the world is best followed by being anxiously engaged in the Lord's work. Hence, there is a counterpart to pausing too long on the edge of the pool of baptism *before entering*—and that is pausing at poolside too long *on the way out*. Reactivated members who have paused on the porch of the Church must not next pause in the foyer. The Holy Ghost can be our constant companion and will confirm our new course, if we so desire. He is prepared to be more than just an occasional friend.

So many people are deflected disciples who merely believe in believing without realizing it isn't faith we need, it is focused faith—faith in the Lord Jesus Christ. Unfocused virtue, unfocused love, or unfocused feelings are like patches of colors as compared with a great painting. To pursue the analogy, admittedly we need to have colors in order to be able to paint, but the discipline involved then requires us to move the various colors from the palette to the canvas. This discipline cannot be achieved if we cling to the way of the world. Worldly ways may permit us for a season to have fleeting religious feelings—but only as long as we do nothing with them. Later on, if we do not focus these feelings, we will lose the capacity to feel at all. The wholesome feelings people have of a religious nature are a preamble to particularity, but that's all. They have the same relationship vagueness has to specificity.

Perhaps one illustration of the need for particularity will help. To speak vaguely as many do of the day of true peace when people "shall beat their swords into plowshares, and their spears into pruning hooks" is most often done by ignoring the preamble to that marvelous promised peace. Isaiah was precise whereas some who quote him are vague, for Isaiah made it abundantly clear that several specific and dramatic conditions must be established first, and then the Lord will "judge among the nations, and shall rebuke many people." (Isaiah 2:4.)

There is a difference in the example at hand between vague yearning and real hope for peace. The former approach assumes that somehow—perhaps through international bodies—the marvelous day of peace will

4

come. The latter view takes account of what else Isaiah said: how the Lord's house shall first be established in the tops of the mountains; how people from all nations shall flow unto it; how out of Zion will go the law; and how out of Jerusalem the word of the Lord. (Isaiah 2:2-3.) Then there will be the Lord's judgment among the nations and His rebuking of many. Those are very specific preambles to the peace promised.

Thus that millenarian moment will not spring out of senates, will not be propelled by mortal proclamations, and will not be traceable to treaties. Rather, the King, Jesus Christ, will have first established His kingdom and His people, physically and spiritually, and He will then come and judge all societies according to His standards, not secular standards.

It is a prophetic promise as specific as it is dramatic—a much different thing than just sloshing around in sentiment, hoping vaguely that the peace spoken of will come in spite of everything.

So far as widespread peace is concerned, it will come not by a never-never gradualism, but by a gradual preparation of a particular people, followed by a sudden—but not unannounced—coming of the King of Peace. No wonder His disciples should seek to establish His righteousness and kingdom! We must be willing to let go of the world in order to save it!

Those who stand indecisively at the foot of the gospel's gangplank, not wishing to come aboard, are, of course, not in the same circumstance as those who accept the gospel as soon as they hear it, though they hear it late in the day. Those later workers, as the Lord Himself tells us, get the same wages as those who signed on early. But those who simply mill about the dockside grumbling about the fare or questioning the seaworthiness of the vessel, instead of helping out, are those most to be pitied.

Since there are no instant Christians, to withhold what we can do to accelerate the process of the perfection of Zion until Zion is nearly perfected is to misconstrue mortality. To withhold all (or even much) of our fellowship, our talents, or our tithing until the Church and its people meet our "high" standard is like trying to book passage on Noah's ark without driving a nail in a plank. We simply walk on board and ask to be shown to our stateroom and inquire as we enter the stateroom about what time dinner is served at the Captain's table! We must sign on for the voyage with all our imperfections, and commit to help each other.

Christ didn't wait to mount the cross to sacrifice Himself until He was guaranteed that all people would appreciate and accept His gift and His message. To try to impose conditions on our service to God is to ignore the reality that only unconditional surrender is acceptable.

Perhaps the holdouts are seeking to strike a special bargain with God, a sort of salvation by snobbery. Those who have so much to give, but will not, may enjoy the attention of anxious loved ones or may even see themselves as being heroic holdouts. But their stubbornness of soul will not create new options; neither will the passage of time. Perhaps these people are somewhat ashamed of the gospel or the church of Jesus Christ and His people. They might try to board the ark unnoticed late at night, but only if the water keeps rising.

Though the pressures to hold on to the world have never been greater, there have never been more obvious reasons for letting go of worldly ways that are increasingly full of despair, decay, and death.

Winston Churchill used a special motto for the last volume of his memoirs of World War II that celebrated the victory of the Allies. Churchill's motto was: "How the great democracies won the war and thus were able to resume the follies which had so nearly cost them their lives." Deafness to secular history is dangerous with its muted memories of past errors. Deafness to scriptural history is fatal.

When Jesus first began to preach strong doctrines (the scriptures refer to these as "hard sayings"), many of those who followed Him "went back, and walked no more with him." (John 6:66.) Once His doctrines really began to make demands of people, it was too much for many.

There are equivalent "hard sayings" about our secular societies that one hesitates to utter but which need to be heard. They are not popular. They have been spoken of before, of course, but repetition does not make something false. A truth may touch us, bore us, or merely make us uncomfortable. But those are reactions to truth, and reactions do not alter the reality of truth itself. Here are a few such hard sayings about our society that, when pondered, may make it easier to let go of the world.

First, there is, whether or not we wish to acknowledge it, an ecology that pertains to human nature just as there is an interrelatedness pertaining to nature. This ecology embodies certain laws which, if violated, will produce certain harsh consequences. These laws pertaining to human nature are as irrevocable as the laws of nature. Sever one tendon of truth and other sinews are weakened. Let one attribute atrophy and others slacken.

Second, for many reasons, work is a spiritual necessity. It would be so even if it were not an economic necessity, but work ploddingly continues to be an economic necessity. Someone has said that idleness is not in itself a vice, but a rust that attacks all virtues. In Ezekiel, we read that one of the sins of Sodom was an "abundance of idleness" made possible, apparently, by some affluence or "fulness of bread." (Ezekiel 16:49.) Worthy work is, of course, a method of producing the goods and services man needs. Justification enough. Additionally, work can give us a sense of creativity and causality. Work also responds to our instinct for usefulness. Further, it provides us with needed satisfactions that we may get in no other way. Moreover, work helps us to avoid boredom. These are not trivial considerations in a sometimes bored and alienated society.

When working productively is the norm, we avoid the social friction that occurs when the idler eats the

7

bread of the worker. The idler comes to expect from, and demands more of, the worker—with resentment building all the time in the worker. Paul reminded the Saints in Thessalonica that he had commanded them as follows: "If any would not work, neither should he eat." (2 Thessalonians 3:10.) He stressed throughout his preachings that "every man shall bear his own burden." (Galatians 6:5.) Somehow, the threat "give me more or I'll take it anyway" can never be fully camouflaged.

One of the reasons some people today feel alienated is that they are alienated from one of the great satisfactions of life—work! Acknowledged is our need to help the poor, but to help in a way that is truly helpful. The more we institutionalize our efforts to help the poor, the less personal these efforts become. The dole desensitizes both the giver and the receiver and it pushes people apart.

Third, idleness combined with lasciviousness further desensitizes us. Paul described a group of people who had been "alienated from the life of God" and who had reached a point where they were "past feeling." (Ephesians 4:18-19.) There is an interconnectedness of such things. When we speak of acting according to the dictates of our conscience, we need to remember that a conscience stilled by sin won't insist upon very much that is right.

We shall find, for instance, that the major things we need and desire, such as identity, community, individuality, creativity, family, and chastity, are ecologically entwined. Because they are bound up together, real liberty does not exist apart from these and other considerations. At a time, for instance, when the institution of the family is under attack, we need to remember what G. K. Chesterton, the able Catholic writer, had to say about how only individuals who understand the value of the family will ultimately be in a position to criticize the state when the state goes awry.

For the state to seek to supplant the family subtly or directly is the equivalent of a spreading oil slick on a reservoir or a bird refuge; it is an enormous error, for when the state spills and spreads, the damage is deep and lasting.

We will find further that we cannot diminish belief in the reality of the resurrection without diminishing the individual's sense of accountability to anybody. People think they are less accountable in the dark, as the behavior of thousands of New Yorkers in the blackout in the summer of 1977 so sadly demonstrated. Those who are so parochial as to think that what is unseen cannot be unethical neglect the reality that there are always at least His two piercing eyes watching. Immortality and accountability are inseparably connected just as surely as the lack of deserved self-esteem is connected with the way in which an individual treats his family, his neighbors, his employees, and so forth.

Fourth, among the hard realities about societies is the reality that liberty, if it is abused too much, will destroy itself. A society that continually permits anything will lose everything. To be sure, drawing lines is admittedly difficult, but once society shrinks from drawing *any* behavioral lines simply because to do so is difficult, it has surrendered. To confuse tolerance with permissiveness can be fatal, since it is like not knowing the difference between a mushroom and a poisonous toadstool.

How many fewer devotees of the First Amendment would there be if, for instance, there were not so much profit in pornography? The words of Isaiah may have some special application to our time. He foresaw a time when, he said, some would call "evil good, and good evil." "Woe," he said, to those who "for reward" would seek to "take away the righteousness of the righteous." (Isaiah 5:20, 23.)

We must never make the error of assuming that the wicked believe in tolerant pluralism—in a "live and let live" philosophy. Misery may crave company, but darkness detests light. Evil people are not polite pluralists—they are predators, as Lot found out in Sodom. Hitler's hatred of the Jews did not remain a private gripe.

Private immorality finally makes itself manifest publicly.

Liberty and order seem always to be in a situation of uneasy balance. As two wise historians, Will and Ariel Durant, said, "If the hunger for liberty destroys order, the hunger for order will destroy liberty." How ironical it would be if, in its headlong and heedless pursuit of various freedoms, our society were only to end up being imprisoned within the high walls of appetite. A self-constructed cell is still a cell.

When David sinned by conspiring to murder Uriah so that he might have Uriah's wife, he sinned gravely. A prophet said that what David had done he had done "because he had no pity." (2 Samuel 12:6.) There was neither pity nor compassion in a desensitized David. What happened to one man can happen to a whole society. Few things are more pitiful than a people who are without pity and who are empty of empathy. The hardness that produces insensitivity toward large-scale abortions will not confine itself to one expression: the insensitivity will spread; it will find other focal points.

The interconnectedness of these things is true of negative things as well as positive things. For instance, once we breach the constraining commandments, there is no place, no other high ground, on which to make a new stand or to regroup society's forces. Is there something wrong about pornography for children that ceases to operate when the consumer becomes eighteen? Of course not! If one abortion is okay, then why not twenty? Once society loses its capacity to say firmly that certain things are wrong *per se,* then it finds itself forever building temporary defenses, drawing new lines, falling back further, and losing its nerve. What starts out as some minor adjustments in the borders of beliefs turns into a rout.

The author wishes he could escape the impression that so many who see themselves as liberated are only "liberated" from light. He wishes that the advice to take up new life-styles did not come so often from flawed failures who seek escape from former roles they could not or would not manage. But worst of all is the shrill insistence that others must do likewise. What starts out as a plea for freedom for a few to live differently soon ends up as a demand for all to be the same. Such misguided individuals—crusaders without the cross—are determined to "redeem all mankind, that one soul shall not be lost." (Moses 4:1.) We listened to that determined approach once before, a very long time ago, when, in the pre-earthly existence, it was rejected.

There are even more reasons to let go of the world.

The interaction between the worlds of children, youth, and adults is a constant reality of life. Predatory behavior knows no borders. If something is considered right for consenting adults (but which is actually wrong), how can advocates argue consistently that it is really wrong for near-adults? Boys, for instance, learn how to be men by watching their fathers. Are we really prepared to perpetuate such problems, generation upon generation? Paternal sanction of pornography merely suggests delay before certain appetites are appropriate—*not* that the appetites are wrong regardless of age. But is an appetite safe only later in life when the danger of its being acted out is greatest? If adults have "caved in" to concupiscence, how free are youth to decide themselves? Evil adults make up more minds than just their own minds.

Of course, we are free to obey or not to obey God's commandments, but we are not free to alter the content of those commandments. Neither can we avoid the consequences of breaking those commandments. Choosing should always include wanting the consequences of what we want.

Additions or amendments to the Ten Commandments would come from the same Source as the original commandments. One of the commandments, for instance, does *not* read, "Thou shalt not commit adultery except between consenting adults." It says, "Thou shalt not commit adultery." Where standards are concerned, ambivalence begets ambivalence, and equivocation begets equivocation. A ruthless society that will not draw any meaningful lines of restraint faces a chartless future.

Some of the very people who warn about the interconnectedness of things in nature are oblivious to the ecology that pertains to human nature. If it were not so tragic, it would be comic—like a child molester or an incestuous parent taking to the soap box to warn us sternly to think of future generations, since strip mining can scar the landscape!

Once the gospel grove sheltered by tall and stalwart redwoods has been abandoned, where will society seek shelter from the storms? In the sagebrush? In the reeds of rationalization? Hypocrisy at least is an attempt to hide shame, but today the very flaunting of certain behavior indicates that our deterioration is reaching some advanced stages. Boldness is not always courage, and when some things come out of the closet, they bring the darkness with them.

Fifth, a hard saying that republics and democracies need to take into account is that there is also an ecology in human rights. Whether we like it or not, our rights of free speech are tied more to other rights, including our property rights, than we may know. Benjamin Franklin anticipated the First Amendment in something he said nearly half a century before its adoption: "This sacred privilege is so essential to free Governments, that the Security of Property, and the Freedom of Speech always go together; and in those wretched Countries where a Man cannot call his Tongue his own, he can scarce call any Thing else his own."

When numerical majorities move relentlessly and heartlessly, they roll over the rights of minorities. Our Republic assumes and requires a certain generosity of spirit among its citizens. That there will be collisions of opinions and views is granted, even expected, but we must lubricate our conflicts within constitutional constraints and within the system of the peaceful play of power. If violence comes to presume a preeminence, as it did in the days of Noah, and if generosity diminishes, except for generosity with other people's goods, then we are in a bad way.

Sixth, our democracy rests upon "obedience to the unenforceable," for self-discipline is as crucial in democracy as in religion. S. M. Lipset has warned us: "Freedom, the underlying principle of a democratic society, requires a commitment to restraint. . . . It is no accident that the Bill of Rights is worded not positively, but largely in the language of restraint." (*The Public Interest.*)

In a similar observation Samuel P. Huntington has warned: "The vulnerability of democratic government in the United States thus comes not primarily from external threats, though such threats are real . . . but rather from the internal dynamics of democracy itself in a highly educated, mobilized, and participant society. 'Democracy never lasts long,' John Adams observed. 'It soon wastes, exhausts, and murders itself. There never was a democracy yet that did not commit suicide.' That suicide is more likely to be the product of overindulgence than of any other cause."

Indulgent democracy produces bureaucracy and apathy. Bureaucracy and apathy are not exclusively democratic diseases, but we are not immune to these strains of political virus.

It is no accident that the scriptures have preserved for us certain precious insights about the times in which Noah lived. Those were times, we read, that were "filled with violence" (Genesis 6:11), and corruption abounded. There was apparently a sense of self-sufficiency, a condition to which Jesus called attention. (Matthew 24:36-41.) Jesus said this condition would be repeated in the last days. The people of Noah's time were desensitized to real dangers. So we may become in our time. Noah and those with him had to let go of their world or perish with it!

It need not be said of our America, or any nation, what Churchill said of his own England in 1936: "I have

13

watched this famous island descending incontinently, fecklessly, the stairway which leads to a dark gulf. It is a fine broad stairway at the beginning, but after a bit the carpet ends. A little farther on there are only flagstones, and a little farther on still, these break beneath your feet." (*While England Slept.*)

One cannot write things such as this introductory chapter without wondering why such plain and simple observations even need to be made. To speak of such things is surely to speak of the obvious, but the obvious often eludes so many. As the ways of the world grow uglier, its appeal, for some, strangely increases.

We often speak of nations being subdued by surprise, but being surprised is often the function of desensitization, of failure to take account of trends and warnings, and of an unwillingness to apply proven principles to remedy wrongs. It will take great courage for us to do what we must do individually to let go of the world, to resist the trends, and to try to turn the trends around. Some pendulums do not swing back automatically; they must be pushed.

Dr. Harold M. Voth, senior psychiatrist and psychoanalyst at the Meninger Foundation, observed in a speech with regard to the interrelatedness of things that "the heterosexual relationship and the family are in peril and so is the nation." He also called attention to the fact that so many of the feminist movements are based upon "an underlying envy of man." No movement based on envy can succeed.

We cannot count on a society increasingly slipping into homosexuality to be on its guard against homosexuality. The more normal abnormalities become, the less reason people have for being wary of them. Various movements involving sex and drugs, and even some involving music, once basically an effort to flee and to escape, have now taken the offensive.

We need to have compassion and love for those who are trying to escape the world. We need to try to understand them and the root causes for their behavior. What we do not need to do, however, is to follow them. They are to be pitied and understood, not praised nor followed.

With the avalanche of abortions in our society, we often speak, and rightfully so, of the rights of the unborn to life. There is another searching issue: the right of the unborn to come into a world in which there is sufficient liberty and opportunity for them to use their agency and to make their decisions accordingly. Dr. Allen Bergin first called to the author's attention the reality that certain societies could become so corrupt that the children born in them had in effect no freedom except to follow in the corrupt paths and channels so strongly grooved in that society.

It was President John Taylor who said of the destruction of Sodom and Gomorrah that "it was better for them to die, and thus be deprived of their agency, which they abused, than entail so much misery on their posterity, and bring ruin upon millions of unborn persons." (*Government of God*, p. 53.) The quality of life includes not simply the quality of air and water and physical environment, but a quality of life in which children can both be born free and be free later to opt for righteousness if they so choose. A decadent society does not offer that prospect.

The more coarse and crude people become, the less they are aware of it. It is safe to assume that the Sodomites regarded themselves as having a certain sophistication. They no doubt made some condescending comments about poor old Lot who did not know what he was missing. A predator does not know he is a predator, for he is "past feeling."

Without the gospel's explanation of life and without the critical data about the plan of life, existence will soon seem like an empty maze. Many so-called great thinkers have exhausted themselves in search of life's meaning and purpose only to conclude there is none. But the futility of life lamented by some is simply a report on their having chosen the wrong conceptual corridor; they generalize beyond their data. Saturated in self-pity, after such narrow searching, sin then becomes a way of confirming the sinner's existence with its pronounced emphasis on celebrating feelings—"I feel, therefore, I am." But sin only further alienates the sinner from the sense of life and its purpose and finally from the capacity to feel itself.

Thus pride and sin keep so many—like the prodigal son—from coming home. Fortunately, the prodigal came to himself—and so do many, for there is a straight and narrow path in the midst of the mortal maze.

But the ways of the world can be turned from only if the correct corridor is to be found.

Surely Paul anticipated a sad trend regarding people's acceptance of Jesus, which accounts for so many moderns who are stranded in the maze. The trend is one in which Christ is credited with a significant ministry in this life but in which his literal resurrection is denied. Paul spoke boldly, declaring, "If in this life only we have hope in Christ, we are of all men most miserable." (1 Corinthians 15:19.) A Christianity that focuses on an *unrisen* Christ is a callow contradiction and it produces a special misery among its adherents, for such faith, Paul said, is "vain; ye are yet in your sins."

Is this dilution of doctrine not what has happened to so much of so-called Christianity with its existential emphasis? An unrisen Christ could never lift all men up! To take the name of Christ to preach against His (and the universal) resurrection is treason of the highest order. Sadly, the name of Christ is often appropriated to fight the work of Christ. Yet possessed of an abiding testimony of the resurrection, modern disciples, like those of old, too can say: "We are troubled on every side, yet not distressed; we are perplexed, but not in despair; Persecuted, but not forsaken; cast down, but not destroyed." (2 Corinthians 4:8-9.)

Those who "in this life only have hope in Christ" will be miserable. Without the resurrection there is no ultimate hope, which brings proximate despair. If death is still victorious, how meaningful is life, after all? If Christ cannot help me, then why follow Him? Hence, in torturing the truth about Christ, mortals only torture themselves. A denial of the divinity of Jesus and His literal resurrection leads many to an existential philosophy that appropriates the name of Christ for a religion that finally slumps into a Sadducean stance. How ironic, how cruel! Thus another compelling reason to reject the world is its telestial theology about Christ.

Of course, we will be impaled upon incredible ironies in our time, but saints of steel can handle irony. A perceptive writer observed of one such irony that "emancipation has to do with power, not love; and a view of life in terms of emancipation—or liberation—will tend to be a political view, or, at least, it will interpret life with a political metaphor." The doctrines of this emancipation stress terms like " 'self-awareness,' 'self-fulfillment,' 'self-discovery,' 'self-determination,' and 'self-sufficiency'— terms that crowd anybody other than the 'self' right out of one's imagination." No wonder such trends result in more and more people living alone, more divorces, and fewer individuals getting married.

The writer noted also an "inevitable fraying of the net of connections between people at many critical intersections, of which the marital knot is only one. Each fraying accelerates others. A break in one connection, such as attachment to a stable community, puts pressure on other connections: marriage, the relationship between parents and children, religious affiliation, a feeling of connection with the past—even citizenship, that sense of membership in a large community which grows best when it is grounded in membership in a small one. . . ." (*New Yorker,* August 30, 1976.)

Emancipation carried to excess is typical of telestial trends that usually lack any inner controls. Only the Lord's way balances our need for liberty and belonging. If we cling to the world, we will have neither!

In such times we should not be dismayed if others do not hear and see what we hear and see. When the voice of God was heard, as recorded in the gospel of John, everyone did not understand it was the voice of God. Some thought that it was thunder. (John 12:29.) Many people can see the same spiritual signal, perceive the same social indicator, but some may be imperceptive and insensitive enough. They fail to understand the significance of what is seen and heard.

One cannot survive in such an age either if he tries to build his spirituality with mere fragments of the faith, with doctrinal debris from other ages. He must have the whole truth (and nothing but the truth) as the foundation stones of his spirituality. Otherwise, he can become very confused about what truly matters.

Thus in letting go of the world and then passing through the gate of repentance and baptism, *all is not done.* There are still old reflexes to be mastered, familiar thoughts that must be turned away, and feelings to be tamed. Our personality must be both gentled and emboldened. There are caterpillar-like challenges waiting to be turned into butterfly-like blessings. There is always time to be managed in order to obtain from our hours the highest and best use. There is the challenge of peer approval, for even with good peers, their approval must not be substituted for His approval should there be a shade of difference.

Indeed, in order to achieve the "mighty change of heart," we must reconstruct that heart. Baptism, properly entered into, can wash away sins in a moment, but the Holy Ghost may need to school us for a lifetime to obtain patience or to dissolve some of the devilish drives within us. Hence there can be no clinging to the world, for clinging will delay, if not destroy, our new-found discipleship. Satan will wait to catch us off guard. He will feed our frustrations.

As we enter church activity, our very consciousness of our shortcomings can be an encouraging sign, for we are no longer content with ourselves as we are. When we begin to be serious about joy, then will be the time that we are most apt to note its absence. There is a danger, however, that this healthy, divine discontent will degenerate into discouragement.

In our guilt there is also a glimmer of hope, for when wrongness is sensed, then there is a chance for goodness.

Pressing forward along the path means trying the experiment of the goodness of the gospel laws, one by one, for it is by obedience to these laws that the needed blessings come. We get the joys of temple work by doing temple work. We get the satisfactions of doing missionary work by doing missionary work.

Does all this mean that in letting go of the world, it will be easy to set priorities? No! It is often harder, for now we choose, *not* between task A, which is a tainted task, and B, which is good; but now we must allot time and talent between C, which is important and good, and D, which is good and important.

The light at the end of the tunnel of time is the light of Christ. Happily, while in the darkness of that same tunnel of time each of us is given, at the start of the journey, a portion of the light of Christ.

It is all a little like a tourist's journey through Hezekiah's tunnel in Jerusalem. We know there is a beginning and an end, for others who have made the journey before so witness. But it is up to us during our journey through the tunnel not to extinguish our own little candle, lest the terror of that tunnel smother our hope and our reason. Soon the light at the end of the tunnel begins its glimmer, and then becomes so bright mortal eyes blink. So it is with life. MacDonald said rightly that "Christ is the way out, and the way in." (*An Anthology* [London: Geoffrey Bles, 1970], p. 71.)

There is a difference between gradual personal progress and dallying with discipleship. The Great Shepherd will seek to keep us all moving along, but when we seek to stray, MacDonald reminds us, the Great Shepherd has sharp-toothed sheep dogs that will be sent to thwart us.

It is a measure of God's love for us, after we have entered the first gate, that the Lord will strive with us, lest we become "entangled again in the vanities of the world." (D&C 20:5.) The only way to avoid being overcome by the cares of the world, therefore, is to stop caring for the world. We must let go of the old world and not look back, and this is so much easier if we press forward with a steadfastness in Christ.

Part of pressing forward consists of not slackening because others refuse to do likewise. Some use the size of the Church as an excuse not to explore it. The Church does not become more true when more people join it (only more glorious in scope)—nor does it become less true when some choose to leave it. Validity has nothing to do with numbers, as the eight on the ark and the three who successfully fled Sodom will testify.

I once heard a nonmember critic of the Church say with refreshing honesty that the Book of Mormon was one of the few books people didn't feel obligated to read before they reviewed or criticized it. He was quite right. In like manner, for some strange reason, it appears to be equally difficult to get some people to study the doctrines of the Church carefully. They would rather dispose of the Church institutionally if they can. That is, if they can readily assume that some of the allegations made against the Church are true, then they feel such are reason enough to dispose of the doctrines of the Church without having to examine them. Those who nurse and care so tenderly for their pet peeve about the Church will find that their pet peeve will bite the hand that feeds it.

It was George MacDonald who warned us about the dangers of dismissing truths because they emanated from some "ism." That is true of Mormonism. To dismiss its doctrines because it is an "ism," without examining those doctrines, is grossly unfair and intellectually dishonest. The doctrines of the atonement or of the preexistence, for instance, must be examined *per se.* They may not be dismissed because of concerns over who may, in fact, hold the priesthood.

It is fashionable, of course, to pervert the process of

examination so that the doctrines of the Church are ignored. It is easy for some to disagree with a particular tactical involvement of the Church on a given issue of the day, but they deprive themselves of the doctrines of the Church that they could come to appreciate and come to get a testimony of, if they really seriously examined them.

The Lord has told us that truth is independent in that sphere in which He has placed it. Each doctrine of the Church carries within itself its own power, its own beauty, and its own witness that it is true, but these doctrines must be explored with real intent. The serious student of art does not loiter around the lobby of the Louvre.

I am reminded of an infantry inspection I once went through in World War II in the Philippines. For days, all of us tried to spruce up the area, to polish our rifles, to shine our shoes, and to make sure that the grounds around our tents were spotless, so that we could undergo a very scrutinizing inspection by a visiting three-star general. Imagine our dismay when on inspection day all of us were lined up and the general merely drove by in a jeep at 35 miles an hour on a road that was at least 100 yards from the place where all the companies in the regiment were lined up! Yet that is about the same way some people inspect and examine the gospel of Jesus Christ and The Church of Jesus Christ of Latter-day Saints. Unbelievers run terrible risks, however, for if they come any closer and try the gospel's goodness, they may like it.

To make up one's mind about the Church as a bystander is to make a fatal mistake. One cannot appreciate holy things without being inside them. Those who recognized Peter on the night of Christ's arraignment did not see Peter in his finest hour; for them to have made a decision about the validity of Christianity on the basis of that one encounter would have been a fatal mistake. The Peter they saw was a Peter in process. His stage of growth had very little to do, however, with

21

the validity of the Sermon on the Mount or the reality of the resurrection that was impending.

Likewise, to watch the Church in action is to see it function at times with imperfect and inexperienced leaders at some levels and with imperfect and inexperienced members at various levels. Finesse is desirable but not always possible. To induce prospective disciples to judge eternal things, therefore, only by noting derisively the spiritual level of some Church members, without examining the doctrines, is Satan's constant tactic to make certain people are not drawn to the truth. To refuse to deal with the doctrines of the Church at least carefully, if not sympathetically, is to deny oneself access to a most glorious experience. But some so do, and we must press forward anyway.

It is possible to have a mediocre people possessed of perfect doctrines. Indeed, perfect doctrines are necessary to change our mediocrity. But the reverse is impossible. One will not find a perfect people with mediocre doctrines!

Nephi lamented the fact that so many people will not "understand great knowledge." (2 Nephi 32:7.) Complexity is scarcely the cause, for the gospel is so plain and simple. Rather, the failure to comprehend seems to be rooted in a resolute refusal to let go of the world long enough to ponder the precious truths in the message of the Master. Because real religion restructures one's understanding of the universe, life, his neighbor, and himself, that restructuring is resisted by many (and almost wildly by some) who sit within humanism's house of cards or cling to sin's status quo.

Thus so many spend their lives in collecting trivial truths and pedestrian knowledge and will not search knowledge, nor understand great knowledge, when it is given unto them in plainness, even as plain as word can be. Caught up in collecting creature comforts, preferring the inconsequential, craving carnally convenient codes, such individuals mute—or misunderstand entirely—the great adventure of the mortal estate. Such people will also be unprepared for the unending estate that follows for us all.

Only minutes away for a few, weeks for others, and no more than years for any of us—that better world is worth pressing forward for. The scriptures are before us, and they testify to us that the closer past travelers have come to it, the greater the glimpse of it, the more glad the eye and the more quickened the pace. Such men and women have witnessed by how they have walked the straight and narrow path; indeed, their very stride is a sermon to us.

Chapter Two

ON INITIATING DISCIPLESHIP AND PRESSING FORWARD

As to trials, why bless your hearts,
the man or woman who enjoys the spirit
of our religion has no trials; but the
man or woman
who tries to live according to the Gospel
of the Son of God, and at the same time
clings to the spirit of the world,
has trials and sorrows acute
and keen, and that, too, continually.
(*Discourses of Brigham Young,* p. 348.)
The city of Enoch was not
prefabricated and put up in a day.
The city was built incrementally and
spiritually as the individuals
in that city were built
incrementally and spiritually. That
near-celestial culture was constructed only as
individuals were improved.

President Brigham Young, five times before coming to the Salt Lake Valley, left or lost everything he had pertaining to this world's goods. Having coped well, he urged us to meet our trials cheerfully, for these will come with initiating discipleship and with letting go of the world.

So many have more than necessary difficulty in initiating and then facing up to both the designation and the duties that come with discipleship. Some seek to run from it altogether. Others refuse to accept the need to try to respond wholly to the full demands of discipleship. Still others close their eyes to discipleship's immense possibilities and opportunities. Why is there such reluctance and ambivalence? Let us focus on several factors and then become prescriptive.

First, there is the seeming improbability and irony of it all! On our own small scale (like Enoch, Moses, and others), we wonder if it really could be that God has chosen us, as a people or individually. Feeling unworthy, unready, and uncertain about what we can contribute, when so called, is different from questioning the call itself, however.

Note the dagger of doubt, "If thou be the Son of God," that Satan hurled at Jesus, seeking to strike at the Savior's identity. The same dagger was flung both on the Mount of Temptation and at Calvary. "He saved others, let him save himself." "Save thyself," they said mockingly. "If thou be the Son of God, come down from the cross." All this was said while legions of angels were at hand! But Jesus knew who He was, and He did not doubt nor retreat from the reality of His role.

Those daggers of doubt will be flung at us. Though far, far less precious prey, we are still fair game. Satan will strike at our identity as disciples of Jesus, appealing to our doubts and misusing our modesty. He will try to transform uncertainty about our adequacy into uncertainty about our callings.

We must beware of this torturing tactic, especially since we are aliens in a strange and increasingly cruel culture. We will feel less and less at home in this world. Though we are—so clearly—not as perfect as Jesus, we can be like Joseph in Egypt, faithful to fundamentals, including our identity. Like Joseph, we can then help the very people who fail to see (or who even scoff at) our role and identity. The more of mankind who can experience us as brothers, the greater the chance for them to come to know the Father.

There is irony also in the sense of the unexpected and

the unlikely being what actually is. Imagine, a maligned, miniscule group of mortals expected to be the light of the world! It has been true of others in centuries past, of course. Now you and I in our own little circles have been placed here to light up the landscape of life for others, frail and flickering as our own flames seem at times.

Fishing nets must be left; hands must be put to the plow 'midst meditating, pondering, and even awe. We, the weak things of the world, should scarcely expect to feel other than weak when arrayed against the world. We will even be seen as both weak and foolish by those we are to help. Hence the need for us to be bold: "Use boldness, but not overbearance; and also see that ye bridle all your passions, that ye may be filled with love; see that ye refrain from idleness." (Alma 38:12.) We can be bold without being overbearing. Only if we control our passions can we be filled with love and be anxiously engaged rather than idle.

Some will attempt to wear us down and intimidate us, especially after initial commitment. Journalists who were covering Napoleon's return from exile reportedly were worn down through intimidation: "The monster has escaped from his place of exile." "The Corsican werewolf has landed at Cannes." "The tyrant has reached Lyon." "The usurper has dared to advance within 150 miles of the capital." "Tomorrow Napoleon will be at our gates." "His Majesty is at Fontainebleau." We must not let ourselves be worn down by the world either through intimidation or temptation.

There is so much that the Church stands for that will, more and more, be confronted by and coexist with evil—cheek by jowl, wheat by tares—until the end comes. Our time will become a calendar of contrasts in which the forces of evil will not only attack righteousness, but will do so with an ersatz enthusiasm and plastic nobility as they do the devil's work. By relentless pressure the adversary will seek to pull all he can into his "outer darkness" forever. It is so like him to direct our attention away from our gravest dangers. Can't you just about hear the preachments against prudery in Sodom and Gomorrah?

Parenthetically, it is also ironical that the adversary has so much influence over some who view themselves as creative. President Brigham Young once said that the adversary never had an idea of his own. Lucifer perverts, not creates, principles; he distorts doctrines. If we want proximity to creativity and individuality in our lives, Lucifer can tell us nothing of such things.

Jesus knew and remembered who He was, on the Mount, in Gethsemane, and on Calvary. Thanks be to God, Jesus did! But mortals who lose their bearings then proceed to lose their souls. No wonder Lucifer seeks to lead us away from the ascending path "carefully" down to hell—a slope so gentle we hardly notice. Adulterers, for instance, don't notice the gradual descent because their minds are on something else. We should not be surprised that we are told that the serpent became the symbol for Satan because the serpent was "more subtle." (Moses 4:5.) It is amazing how often the adversary can induce those being imprisoned by their own appetites to feel exhilaration even as they brick themselves in.

So much for sample ways in which irony and improbability challenge discipleship in a time of changing values.

There is a further factor: the failure to recognize that there is clearly a territory between that of the devil and that of the Lord. It is filled with what the scriptures call "the works of men" and is guided by "the commandments of men." In it, symbolically, heroin addicts are often moved to methadone, the irony being that abstinence is better than any addiction. In some things, abstinence is the Lord's way. Man's way may be better than the devil's way, but it is still inadequate and is not the Lord's way. Man's way equivocates too much with regard to such basics as freedom and family and identity and chastity and fidelity.

So many prospective disciples of Jesus spend their lives in this middle world, confused about which camp they belong to and which cadence they are to march to. It takes real integrity to see this middle world clearly, and the new disciple must not pause in it lest he become confused and remain in that realm.

Now let us consider what must be laid at the door of each of us in terms of our individual accountability to avoid being thrown off by the aforementioned challenges of inadequacy, improbability, and irony, by losing our way and being drawn into the middle world just described.

1. Since Jesus is at the very center of it all, we must make Him and His ways the light by which we steer and the light that we hold up to others. To proceed in any other way is to proceed with less light—much less light. Life is too filled with perplexities and variables for one to prevail without the guiding light of the gospel. The wisdom of men, by itself, is simply not adequate for all circumstances. Too many unintended, unforeseen, and undesired consequences flow from even the most sincere but erroneous efforts. The Spirit can teach of things as they really are, not just as we otherwise imperfectly perceive them.

2. We need to feast upon the words of Christ in the scriptures and as these words come to us from living prophets. Just nibbling occasionally will not do. (See 2 Nephi 31:20 and 32:3.) Feasting means partaking with relish and delight and savoring—not gorging episodically in heedless hunger, but partaking gratefully, dining with delight, at a sumptuous spread carefully and lovingly prepared by prophet-chefs over the centuries. These words plus the gift of the Holy Ghost will tell us all things we should do. The scriptures, ancient and continuing, are the key of knowledge. When Jesus was indicting the lawyers, he said (as added in the Inspired Translation of the Bible) that they had lost the key of knowledge, which Jesus then defined as "the fullness of the scriptures." (Luke 11:53, Inspired Version.) Not a portion, mind you, but the fullness, including the words of living oracles! Appreciation for and the acceptance of

28

the scriptures and the words of the living prophets are much more important steps than many realize. The Lord has said, ". . . he that will not believe my words will not believe me—that I am." (Ether 4:12.) To turn aside His teachings is to turn away from Him, and disdain for His doctrines is disdain for Him.

3. We need to heed the warnings of the prophets. For instance, President Joseph F. Smith said that three tests would come upon the Church from within: false educational ideas, sexual impurity, and the praise of the world (especially from prominent individuals). Presumably, each test would bring its own variations. President Smith said that of the three, maintaining sexual purity was the most vital: "If purity of life is neglected, all other dangers set in upon us like the rivers of waters when the flood gates are opened." (*Gospel Doctrine,* p. 313.)

4. We need to become more righteous and more abounding in the virtues that Peter enumerated (faith, knowledge, virtue, temperance, patience, godliness, brotherly kindness, and charity). If we become more virtuous, we are given a stunning promise, namely, that we will then be increased in our "knowledge of our Lord Jesus Christ." (2 Peter 1:8.) See how we tie back to Jesus and how growth is tied to goodness?

Jesus once asked His followers on this hemisphere, "Therefore, what manner of men ought ye to be?" He then gave the answer: "Verily I say unto you, *even as I am.*" (3 Nephi 27:27. Italics added.) If we are to be His people, we must be ever and ever more like Him. Only then can we be trusted with power, especially heavenly power.

In this connection, seldom has the Lord been so direct as when He said that many do not learn "this one lesson . . . that the powers of heaven cannot be controlled nor handled only upon the principles of righteousness." (D&C 121:34-36.) Apparently, we have strong tendencies to forget "this one lesson."

5. To be like Jesus, we must cultivate a love of pure

29

intelligence, of light and truth. One way of testing our present commitment—and whether or not our love of light and truth is really unconditional—is to ask ourselves this question: Is my love of light and truth sufficiently strong so that when it (having my errors exposed) happens—and it will—I can cope with the consequences? When the glow of the gospel so illuminates an incident that I see my shortcomings in shame and sorrow, is it with a grateful shame and a godly sorrow that I start scrubbing my soul? Or is the light an inconvenience, an irritation?

This love of light will also help us avoid the tragic error of those who insist upon fondling their failings. For while with light comes discovery of our deficiencies, also with the light of the gospel there comes a brightness of hope.

6. While we hope our righteousness will become more and more reflexive, we must not allow our religion to become routine. It must remain a high adventure. The religion of Rameumptom, the tower folk in the Book of Mormon, was at its center filled with ritual, repetition, and routine. (Note that satanic sameness again.) The Rameumptomites were proud "that they were chosen." You see how, if the adversary can reach us, he can turn even a virtue into a vice?

Satan can play many games with us. First, he seeks to persuade men that there is no God. Failing that, he says if there is a God, rebel against Him. Or, if there is a God, then persuade people to think of Him as a mere life force, impersonal and undemanding.

The worshipers at Rameumptom so ritualized their religion that they never spoke of their God "again until they had assembled themselves together" a week later at the holy stand. (Alma 31:23.) Note the contrast in how Jesus instructed His followers on this hemisphere: "Therefore, go ye into your homes, and ponder upon the things which I have said, and ask of the Father, in my name, that ye may understand, and prepare your minds for the morrow, and I come unto you again." (3 Nephi

17:3.) See how the Master focuses on the family—on pondering, praying, preparing together! It should not surprise us, if we routinize our religion and do not assign the highest priority to the kingdom, that our hearts and minds will quite naturally drift to other things.

God, who will one day provide "a perfect remembrance" of our guilt, "a bright recollection" (Alma 5:18, 11:43), could also, if He so chose, portray perfectly what we could have achieved and what we might have been. It is difficult to assess which of our sins would be most devastating to see: the things *committed* or the things *omitted*. The two are linked. It is so important that we must determine those things we will *not* do in order to be freed to do those things we *will* do.

7. Pondering our performance and our progress is also important. If we extrapolate today's trends in ourselves, do we like what we see? What will be the bottom line of today's behavior if persisted in much longer? Some trends need correcting, others accelerating. How we manage time is often a good measure of our progress along the path.

In the management of time, as in the management of self, the prevention of a problem is best. For instance, a little self-discipline to hold down unnecessary social commitments is better than lame excuses and squirming later on.

Again, what manner of individuals ought we to be? Like Christ! We must move toward that point of which Paul spoke when "we have the mind of Christ." (1 Corinthians 2:16.) That we have a great distance to go should not keep us from continuing the journey. A prophet has promised that the word of God will "lead the man of Christ in a straight and narrow course" and "land their souls at the right hand of God in the kingdom of heaven." (Helaman 3:29-30.)

8. We must cleave to the kingdom. The Church will become, even more, the Savior's societal spearhead, the institutional rallying point for the forces of righteousness. Make no mistake about it.

How glorious it is for us to live in the times that our forefathers "awaited with anxious expectation." (D&C 121:27.) Our time is now. Our ancestors saw this age and yearned for it. Now we are here, talent-laden, surrounded by opportunities and challenges.

The kingdoms of this world will one day "acknowledge that the kingdom of Zion is in very deed the kingdom of our God and his Christ" (D&C 105:32), but only after it has grown *numerically* and *spiritually*. Each of us has a part in accelerating that growth. We were appointed to this age to help bring about those two conditions by using our time, talents, and testimonies. The good life is the best preparation for bad times.

Will there be troubles before that day? Yes, and the Lord has said of us and those troubles, ". . . the saints also shall hardly escape; nevertheless, I, the Lord, am with them." (D&C 63:34.) We must not expect across-the-board immunity from difficulty, but if we are prepared, we shall not fear. (D&C 38:30.) We must not automatically assume that time wounds all heels, for the bad are not always exposed—but eternity *will* bring a fullness of justice.

If in our small way we too must deflect the dagger of doubt—if we are to be disciples—then, also in our own small way, we are entitled to be assured concerning our tasks in this, our time. Jesus said, ". . . for this cause came I into the world." (John 18:37.) Likewise to do our tiny tasks, we have been sent into the world—now!

The rhetorical question posed by Nephi ("I would ask if all is done?"—2 Nephi 31:19) cannot be fully answered until the end. Even for Jesus, completeness came only after Calvary when He said, "It is finished." (John 19:30.) Then joy came with the emptying of the garden tomb and also with His visit to the adjoining hemisphere when He said, "And now behold, my joy is full." (3 Nephi 17:20.) Full joy follows full service, and so much waits to be done.

The costs of discipleship are not paid just once, therefore, at the front end and then all is done. The dues for discipleship continue and are on an ascending scale. If it were not so, prophets would speak of entering only one narrow gate of baptism and then of immediate rest and repose; instead, there are ever so many reminders of the straight and narrow way that leads on and on after the entering of the first gate.

Of course, there is another gate––the final gate to Home. But we are talking about the path between those two gates and the high adventure that ensues even when we are within sight of Home. We do not enter into that rest until the Lord welcomes us inside His kingdom and we are home at last. We are at best barely in the suburbs, and we still have miles to go.

President N. Eldon Tanner has been known to say to others when they seem frayed and overwhelmed by the journey, "You wouldn't want it to be easy, would you?"

Lest the initiate think he is hemmed in because of the straightness and narrowness of the way, that analogy pertains to doctrines and behavior, for there is a wide world with remarkable room for creativity in our service to others and in the application of our God-given talents. Individuals can "do *many* things of their own free will, and bring to pass much righteousness; For the power is in them. . . ." (D&C 58:27-28. Italics added.)

Often ignored in this regard are several revelations that reflect the Lord's response to certain inquiries early in this dispensation. In one case, those who were to undertake a certain mission were told that it did not matter whether they went "by water or by land," for later decisions could be made "according to their judgments hereafter." (D&C 61:22.) In a second case, the Lord invited His disciples to make their own decision as to purchasing or constructing craft––"it mattereth not unto me"––as long as those involved got to St. Louis. (D&C 60:5.) Five days later, the Lord said His disciples could travel in a group upon returning or two by two "as seemeth you good." (D&C 62:5.)

Lest one smile condescendingly at these early followers, it should be recalled that they were accustomed to responding to specific revelations as well as being anxious to do what the Lord wanted. Nor should we pass all this off by simply saying that when we are righteous the Lord will bless us as we travel. While true, that approach neglects things to be learned from these revelations. These revelations do not reflect indifference or impatience, but the Lord's sweet schooling of his disciples. Praying, deciding, and coping are the lot of the believer as he meets with life's complexities and comes to crossroads.

In a later revelation, two missionaries were told that they could set forth to preach the gospel "whether to the north or to the south, to the east or to the west, it mattereth not, for ye cannot go amiss." (D&C 80:3.) Opportunities and options abound all about us to "bring to pass much righteousness." We would be staggered and ashamed if we saw fully the unused and unexplored possibilities for service that surround each of us all of the time.

He is a loving, encouraging, and emancipating Lord who urges us to use our minds and talents in good causes. He who has arranged this planet for us with adequate natural resources ("enough and to spare") has also supplied a surplus of opportunities for the stretching of our souls, if we but desire to do so.

The idea or imagery of pressing forward suggests, therefore, earnestness and energy and not a passive stroll in the general direction of Home and Him. The imagery also emphasizes a direction--forward--not side trips and detours. Detours don't have to be bad to have a bad effect--they always cost us time. They may also mean that we were not there to help a fellow traveler who needed us as he stumbled. Pressing forward suggests an enthusiastic, relentless progress along the path, "with a steadfastness in Christ" (2 Nephi 31:20) being part of the imagery.

Deciding for discipleship does not immunize us against irony, nor does it guarantee an unbroken, uninterrupted ascent on the straight and narrow path.

C. S. Lewis warned the believer—especially the new or renewed believer—that "there will come a moment when there is bad news, or he is in trouble, or is living among a lot of other people who do not believe it, and all at once his emotions will rise up and carry out a sort of blitz on his belief." (*Mere Christianity* [New York: Macmillan, 1976], p. 123.) Our faith must ride out our moods, or our discipleship will be too much at the mercy of mood, men, and circumstances.

One aid in dealing with this sort of test is to study the scriptures. Feasting on the word of Christ can keep us from being mercurial and moody, which is vital not alone for ourselves, but also for our fellow travelers who are depending upon our being steadfast lest they lose their grip, too.

It should neither surprise us nor dismay us that only when we try to become better do we begin to get a fuller notion of how bad we are. Lewis also said, "No man knows how bad he is till he has tried very hard to be good. . . . That is why bad people, in one sense, know very little about badness. They have lived a sheltered life by always giving in." (*Mere Christianity*, pp. 124-25.)

There are those moments as we press forward when we need to remember that the Church is doctrine, organization, ordinances, and authority (and God be praised for these), but the Church is also *us*—people drawn together in our imperfections. We are not yet fully truthful, fully considerate, or fully free from the tendency to manipulate or from sin; we are disciples who need both loving and disciplining. Thus, when we are disappointed, it is with ourselves or other disciples, not with doctrines.

It is, for instance, not likely that a member would come home from a church meeting depressed by the doctrine of the atonement, but rather by the frailty of the flesh in the face of the Divine generosity and grace that abound in the atonement. We are not likely to be irritated by the blessing on the sacrament so much as we might occasionally be jarred in our devotions by an irreverent deacon. We are almost certain to appreciate the authority of the priesthood on which we all depend for blessings and ordinances and for direction in organization; yet sometimes we may let ourselves be offended or irritated by how a holder of that authority misuses his priesthood.

The duality of divinity in the Church and the humanity in its people is something with which discipleship must deal almost daily. It is impossible not to notice and not to be disappointed, at times. But on reflection, is it not true that usually when we complain about "the Church," we are really complaining about ourselves? God could, of course, have kept us out of the Church; it could have been the church of one perfect member—the Church of *Jesus Christ.* Happily for us all, it is The Church of Jesus Christ of *Latter-day Saints!*

Since the Church was given, according to Paul, "for the perfecting of the saints" (Ephesians 4:12), we must expect to feel and see that very process operating in ourselves and in others. There are pain, frustration, disappointment—and development. The impact of this blend of divinity and humanity is unavoidable.

One of the values of rotation in our church assignments is that we can come to appreciate others and what they have done or put up with. There are some roles that call for advocacy and pushing, and one who has been in such a role for a while may need a role that calls for him to develop his skills of reconciliation and mediation. Spiritual symmetry does call, at times, for the knocking off of rough edges and corners; sometimes those are our own edges, while at other times it is our strong stance that peels off someone else's corner. The Savior warned us about the inevitability of offenses—but without excusing those who cause them needlessly.

Of course, one can know all this intellectually and still overreact when it happens personally to us. It is different then—but only because it happened to a different person, "me"! We cannot be increasing our capacity to care and be sharpening our sensitivity to others and to righteousness and fail to notice the fallings short. How can we realistically expect to be in a church comprised of the weak and the foolish (as the world measures such things) and not notice?

There will be irritants that will test new intentions to love and to endure, and such things can be like gravel in the gears of pressing forward. A few examples will illustrate:

1. Being on the underside of someone else's achievement. This error arises from the false sense of our being in competition. It is best to keep score only on one's self. We should be genuinely glad when others succeed; if we cannot at first cheer, then let us at least not sneer.

2. Experiencing a lack of reciprocity in loving and levelling. Love is never wasted, for its value does not rest upon reciprocity. Truth spoken in love may be unappreciated, but it does not thereby become untrue.

3. Being embarrassed by another disciple's efforts, especially when these are duly noted by non- and near-believers. Clumsy conviction is unfortunate and can be costly. But before we fault others for lack of finesse in the fray, we must remember that reticence to enter the fray may be more regrettable.

4. Being overly upset when those we have lovingly and tenderly labored with and sheltered to bring thus far encounter unnecessary shortfalls in the style and substance of those about them in the Church. It is good that we care, but the wrong kind of caring can be convoluted into condescension.

5. Failing to speak up or to show up with resultant guilt over what might have been. We must engage in introspection rather than justification in such moments.

6. Being chagrined when some seem to speak for the Church inaccurately and insensitively. Those who seek to carry the colors will not always be free of runny noses and dirty hands. The deep desire we have to be seen of men only when we are at our best is natural but is sometimes at the mercy of inadequacy and impulse. The only sermons we can really control are those we give—at the

pulpit and in our performance. Best save our squirming for these sermons, even if we must wince occasionally otherwise.

Of meeting and coping with such real and recurring challenges in the kingdom, one basic fact is paramount: There can be no all-purpose handbook to cover all human situations with a page for every problem; each of us must develop his own responses to such dilemmas, and those responses must be given to us by the Holy Ghost, who is the unerring guide in telling us "all things" we need to do.

But other comments are called for too:

First, there is no way that we can be insulated from each other and still develop the skills and strengths required, for the gathering pools our weaknesses as well as our talents. But discipleship is designed to deplete the former while increasing and utilizing the latter.

Second, as far as life in the Church is concerned, counting blessings as well as blemishes will show many more blessings. Besides, changing without chafing is a rare experience, and, happily, so many lives are being changed in the kingdom.

Third, while others can help us in dealing with the challenges cited above, and those like them, we must be careful not to make the fatal error, often made in secular life, of assuming that if there is a problem, then somebody else (probably government) is obligated to solve it. The more we blame things outside ourselves, the greater the tendency to look outside ourselves for solutions. No proxy can press forward for us.

Fourth, while it is only a rare circumstance in which we will have truly used all the remedies available to meet such challenges, there is the equivalent (for us as individuals) of the promise the Lord gave to the Church—that when all that could be done has been done, then matters are in the Lord's hands. He is perfect in his love, mercy, and justice. Meanwhile, though we do not do things "for the record" in the Church, there is a record, and when we have gone the full first mile and a

38

stretching second, such will be duly and divinely noted.

Meanwhile, we had better be very careful about noting and moaning over the motes we see in others. There are so many of our own beams to be moved. There will be, of course, complete accountability for all. If a leader, for instance, offends needlessly, then he is responsible for that error. But those who react to his failure with a failure of their own are likewise accountable. There is as much individual accountability in reactions as in actions.

If we are anxiously engaged in personal improvement, those flaws in others that must be dealt with (for the sake of all) can be approached from a position of strength and security. Correction must be correct. It must also be administered firmly and lovingly--when we are dedicated, not just irritated.

At the risk of detracting from the usual imagery associated with the straight and narrow path, pressing forward seems more like striding in the surf than walking on dry land. If we don't press forward in water, we are quickly taken in another direction. Likewise, men are always in motion, if only in the turbulence of their thoughts; and if the direction is not forward, then there is drifting and trouble, especially when striving to stay on a precise course like the straight and narrow!

Initiation, therefore, requires determination in the development of discipleship. Those who truly seek steadfastness will know the difference between making an announcement of an intention and its accomplishment. The former is sometimes necessary and helpful, but it must never become a substitute for the latter. Those who are increasingly steadfast will find that putting hands to the plow also keeps us from clinging to the world.

In sum, pressing forward requires letting go of the world and quickly initiating discipleship. Then, in recurring sequences shaped by circumstances, it requires being obedient, hoping, studying, being steadfast, loving God and man, and enduring well to the end. Nephi's imagery conveys a zestfulness: pressing forward, having a brightness of hope, feasting upon the words of Christ—an earnest enthusiasm to live righteously. Dullness is undescriptive of such disciples. Bored is the wrong word to describe such believers. Casual is the incorrect connotation for such climbers. Nephi's adjectives are appropriate for the people on this ascending path. It is a journey given to us by Jesus, and it will take all we have. But at the end of it, we will receive all that He has!

Chapter Three

ON BEING OBEDIENT

And Samuel said, . . .
Behold, to obey is better than sacrifice,
and to hearken than the fat of rams.
(1 Samuel 15:22)
Obedience is the opener of eyes.
(George MacDonald, *An Anthology,* p. 42.)
By obeying one learns how to obey.
(Ibid., p. 118.)
So much more can be achieved when there
is overlapping obedience,
as in the case of Abraham and Isaac.
A few tasks in the Church are solitary, but
most often—whether in a missionary
companionship, work on a
welfare farm, or a family genealogical
organization—overlapping obedience gives
a greater impact.
If we knew how often the obedience of others
is affected by our own and how often
our stepping forth soon brings forth a whole
platoon of helpers and how often our
speaking forth soon creates a chorus—we
would be even more ashamed of our slackness
and our silence.

In an age that enthrones education with its many blessings but also with unintended and unnecessary spinoffs of intellectualism and humanism's odd pride in its despair, wherein there has been so much emphasis on self rather than others, obedience and humility have fallen on hard times. Their place on the societal scale of values is low.

This lamentable condition is yet another evidence of how following the fashions of this world poorly equips us for a better world.

It is difficult indeed to press forward if we do not know how to obey. Obedience is not some ritualistic irrelevancy insisted upon by a capricious god, but a rigorous requirement of a loving Father who knows and loves us. But He also knows what is ahead of us.

Disobedience brings despair, and deviation (so often in the name of liberty) brings the loss of freedom. Our minds cannot yet fully comprehend that paradox, but it is there, like it or not.

One of the reasons that "we see through a glass, darkly" (1 Corinthians 13:12) is that our eyes are not fully opened by obedience. We err if we think there is some crash course by which we can learn obedience other than by obedience. There is no virtue that compensates or substitutes for obedience.

Suppose Peter and the others in the fishing boats of Galilee had hesitated to obey the invitation of Jesus to follow Him and become fishers of men? Suppose Peter had asked Jesus to explain this new movement and its political prospects *before* he obeyed? It is in the very nature of things, at times, that understanding follows, not precedes, obeying. Obedience is not blind faith at all, but a wider and deeper seeing with the "eye of faith"; it is a marshaling of our experience from previous obeying and trusting for our new adventures and understandings. In effect, we are saying, "I will try and trust once again. I will go and do what the Lord has commanded." Obedience is, except in our very first experiences, the expression of experience. When combined with the promptings of the Spirit, both will say "Go!" so far as pressing forward is concerned.

One feels sorry for those who will not walk to the edge of the light except on the basis of intellectual commitment. Intellectual commitment is helpful but suffers from its finiteness, from its inability to stretch beyond where the finite mind can take it. Obedience clearly does not disavow the mind, but it does not let the mind limit one's capacity to accept new truths and to cope with new experiences. Obedience springs not from weakness, but from spiritual strength and from a reservoir of affirmative experience, which helps us to trust God for that which we do not yet know.

Obedience permits us to pioneer beyond the past. This obedience exploits experience without being limited by it. What reason concludes are impassable mountains, revelation shows to be rolling hills over which we can pass if we press forward. Sitting and staring at the slopes can make them into stern Sierras. Elder Boyd K. Packer has used a felicitous phrase in this regard that can help us to cope with suffering and problems and then to move on. There are, he has said, times when we must "pick up our handcart and head west."

The fellowship of foreordination puts us in touch with the deep past, with reservoirs of earlier experience of having obeyed and having performed reasonably well. If this life were all there were, there would be no reason to endure pain and deprivation out of a sense of higher duty. Indeed, if this life were all there were, there would be no higher or lower and no sense of duty at all. Disbelievers may rage at the human predicament till hoarse, but their raging does not alter the reality of our premortal experiences or the reality of the resurrection.

Obedience to the divine laws written upon our soul will help us to counter some of the social surges of our time. Wise parents everywhere, for instance, will go on caring about the chastity of their children even when their culture expresses no such concern at all. They will know and understand in ways that words cannot express; they have reasons that are of the heart, and the heart usually holds out longer than the head.

Obedience is the outer expression of our inner gospel gyroscope. Knowing that He will lead us aright, we put our hand in His and trust in Him as we pass through our fiery trials.

There is an important clue in the Old Testament scripture about obeying being better than sacrifice, and to hearken than the fat of rams. Because obedience takes us to higher realms of behavior that lie beyond ritual, it is not for clods, but for the sure-footed adventurers. Obedience suggests a readiness for new and righteous experiences that will be denied those who are still back at the level of sacrifice and ritual. To the unknowing outsider, obedience is seen as a dull, repeated sense of duty. But to the insider, it is a departure point in the development of the soul.

Christ went to the cross out of a sense of obedience and trust, not intellectual insight; being obedient, He could forgo the praise of men, for there was no earthly applause to help Him to carry or to mount the cross.

Obedience suggests a capacity to understand, a mute certainty, even when we are in the midst of being misunderstood. Obedience involves not only dogged determination, but also a sense of anticipation.

Those myopic mortals who do not believe in absolute truths fail to understand that once they have removed God from their thinking, the Core and the Cause of life, they have in effect removed everything else. The grave is not a period terminating meaning and personality—it is a mere semicolon, to cite one such absolute truth.

Paul reminded the Hebrews, and all of us, that Jesus learned obedience by the things which he suffered. (Hebrews 5:8.) Suffering is a hard way to learn, but perhaps the only way for us to learn certain things, for deep insights do not come to an outsider; they come from being inside certain experiences. Obedience permits us to hear things we would not otherwise be able to listen to, because we would so easily be offended. In Proverbs we read that a wise reprover is heard only by "an obedient ear." (Proverbs 25:12.)

The "obedient children" Peter spoke of were individuals who did not go on "fashioning [themselves] according to the former lusts in [their] ignorance." (1 Peter 1:14.) We may be children, but we can be obedient children. Christ calls upon us to be childlike instead of being childish.

We cannot obey, of course, unless we have faith. Paul said that "by faith" Abraham obeyed. (Hebrews 11:8-9, 17.) There is an immense insight given by Paul in his epistle to the Romans in which he praised them and then said, "But God be thanked, that ye were the servants of sin, but ye have obeyed from the heart that form of doctrine which was delivered you." (Romans 6:17.) Obeying "from the heart" is one great key. It is obedience because of the word and not because of imposed circumstances.

Peter observed that our souls can be purified by "obeying the truth." (2 Peter 1:22.) In this dispensation, the Lord said to the Saints, "But behold, they have not learned to be obedient to the things which I required at their hands. . . ." (D&C 105:3.) This suggests the need for us to receive a careful schooling at the hands of our Father in heaven and His Son, Jesus Christ, in which they deliberately require certain things of us so that we might learn obedience. Of the early Twelve of this dispensation the Lord said, "And after . . . much tribulation . . . they shall be converted." (D&C 112:13.) This is the same message given to Peter, who, after conversion, was to strengthen his brethren.

Could it be also that so much depends upon our capacity to be obedient now because our ability to manage power and self is even more so essential in the world to come? Breathtaking assignments can be performed there only if we have developed here the kind of obedience that higher divine laws require of us.

When we can't quite cut ourselves free from those things which draw and hold us to the world, we are not ready yet for the next adventures and new experiences of a high order. Abraham's great adventure with Isaac on Mount Moriah could not have occurred without both his sense of obedience and Isaac's sense of obedience.

Nephi could not have had certain experiences if he had not had that quality of obedience, for he openly strove to follow a perfect pattern, Jesus: "Know ye not that he was holy? But notwithstanding he being holy, he showeth unto the children of men that, according to the flesh he humbleth himself before the Father, and witnesseth unto the Father that he would be obedient unto him in keeping his commandments." (2 Nephi 31:7.) The significance of Jesus' obedience was clearly not lost upon Nephi.

Another key to obedience is whether or not we can cut free from the pleasures of the world. The Lord said, "And your hearts are not satisfied. And ye obey not the truth, but have pleasure in unrighteousness." (D&C 56:15.)

Each of us can now make fresh individual determinations to bless others by the added warmth and light that will flow from us if we are obedient, for all whom we know are immortals—immortals whose role in eternity will depend, in part, upon us and the quality of our obedience to the kingdom!

Those who insist upon too much explaining before obeying are insisting on a complete map instead of trusting in a beckoning Lord. Such individuals would discard the map anyway because they would not be willing to follow it; it would seem too simple, too direct.

Though on an infinitely smaller scale, when each man insists on walking in his own way, he is but mirroring our ego-saturated brother in the premortal world who wanted things his own way. In some twisted contemporary thinking there is likewise a connection between glory and "my way." In any case, to go on insisting on "*my* way" instead of *the* way is to remain unrescued and unhappy.

Rebels forget that their breath and strength come from Him whom they rebel against. So does their free agency. Moreover, their very rebellion and disobedience testify to the existence of a higher standard they refuse to keep—like spoiled children at play, pretending they are "on their own," when their clothes, meals, and home are provided by the very Father whom they rebel against and decry!

Obedience to correct and true principles helps us to overcome this world and fits us for a better world. Obedience gets us through the several passages, like Scylla and Charybdis, that we simply could not navigate alone. Even experienced ships' captains are willing to let a pilot bring their ship to an unknown harbor.

Once through the reefs and shoals, then, is not obedience obsolete? Are we not through the narrow-necked channel of life and safely in the harbor, which is as wide as the universe? Perhaps. But since it is a universe of law in which not only the winds obey His will, but the very galaxies, we should not be so quick to suggest the obsolescence of obedience.

As we strive for obedience, a willing humility has within itself some hidden helping graces of no small significance. By seeing ourselves more realistically, without the inflating effects of egoism, we can have a sense of proportion about ourselves that is denied to the egoist. We are so much freer to examine the ideas and contributions of others with greater objectivity when we do not first compute the costs of their contributions to our role and status. We can be quicker to praise, more certain of our ground when we must demur. There can even be a healthy humor to lubricate relationships in situations of stress.

With humility, our own motives will be less suspect and easier to diagnose. We can more quickly identify the task to be done when we are less concerned about assigning credit. Being more supple in response to the whisperings of the Spirit, we can deal with shades and nuances that escape the egoist.

Further, without humility, the size of our present problems can be easily exaggerated. Has not each of us had a pebble in his shoe that seemed rock-sized, only to have trouble spotting it as the shoe is emptied? Who has not placed his tongue in the hole the dentist is drilling and been persuaded that he has discovered another Grand Canyon?

When we are humble enough to have basic faith, we can, like Nephi, trust the Lord when he gives us an errand, for he will also give us the necessary spiritual and logistical support. Nephi did not demand of the Lord to know all the particulars between initiation and completion. Note the similarity of Nephi's words "I will go and do" (1 Nephi 3:7), in a circumstance involving a committed and able disciple, and the words of the Prodigal Son, a beginning disciple, who at last determined to get back on the straight and narrow path: "I will arise and go. . . ." (Luke 15:18). Such determination is the beginning of discipleship.

With humility, the mind and the heart are both more open. With experience in spiritual things comes even greater humility. As we come to really believe that the Lord is bound when we do what he asks, then we can entertain and act upon still other tasks he gives us with humble assurance—tasks that a short time before would have seemed impossible.

A father who finds it difficult to express his love vocally for his children may need, at first, to be humbly obedient in holding family home evenings in order to help him to discover, or to increase, his appreciation for his children. Next can come to him the courage to say "I love you" to each one. Likewise, obeying and doing are one in other ways. The *partial* tithepayer will never see the "windows of heaven" *fully* open until he fulfills his obligations to the Lord fully and willingly.

Having the humility to plan (and it so easy to misuse moments otherwise) is a part of discipleship. It is reassuring to find how even a few minutes' forethought at daybreak about what the day can hold, or before a meeting about what one wishes to see done or to contribute, can make us much more effective. There is real joy in compliments given spontaneously, yet contemplating how best to compliment another will usually increase the helpfulness and the relevancy of what is finally said.

Obeying now also gives us a fresh vitality, breaking us free from the encirclement of past errors. The Lord, better than anyone, knows our past and what deprivations we may have experienced, but he also knows our possibilities; he will not let the past hold the future hostage. But we must trust him and "try the experiment" of his gospel's goodness. A mere "desire to believe" is a "square one." But he will meet us even there!

When at times we encounter a situation in church service in which a pigeon seems to be supervising an eagle, we need to be accepting even if our evaluation seems accurate. Besides, humility keeps us from spending our time and talent wastefully in counting the plumage of our peers. Remember, this is a kingdom wherein the First is the servant of all! Obedience helps us to serve each other so much better without resentment or condescension.

MacDonald pressed home another reality about obedience that we all need to heed: "A time comes to every man when he must obey, or make such refusal—*and know it* . . . when he will see the nature of his deed, *with the knowledge that he was dimly seeing it so even when he did it:* the alternative had been put before him." (George MacDonald, *An Anthology,* p. 41. Italics in original.)

Just as the black box carried by commercial planes to record what happens in flight can, when recovered after air tragedies, tell so much, so the seismograph of the soul can tell us much about those moments of decision, when we knew what we did was wrong even as we did it, and there will be no gainsaying it, no fobbing it off as a semantical misunderstanding or miscommunication. Our decision was deliberate; the record will clearly show that we took leave of our values and/or our courage.

The young man, apparently a fine young man, who came to Jesus to know what he must do to have eternal life was asked to sell all that he had and give the proceeds to the poor. He had obeyed and kept the other commandments, but went away sorrowing because he could not obey what for him was a stiff requirement. (Matthew 19:16-22.) Given his goodness and other skills, one cannot help but wonder what further he might have done for the kingdom and to what lands and people he might have been sent. But he could not obey!

Obedience can break us free not only from the imprisoning status quo of sin, but also from passive performance in well doing.

In a speech to the Brigham Young University student body in 1962, President Harold B. Lee, then a member of the Council of the Twelve, counseled as follows:

"Some of the greatest religious experiences have come out of some of the most terrifying experiences. . . . Though he were a Son (meaning the Son of God), yet learned he obedience by the things which he suffered; . . . And being made perfect, he became the author of eternal salvation unto all of them that obeyed him. (Hebrews 5:8-9.)" ("Sweet Are the Uses of Adversity," *BYU Speeches of the Year,* February 7, 1962.)

In that same speech President Lee, after noting how, at times, "the Lord doth chasten his people with many afflictions" so that his people would remember him, added, "Isn't that sad?" Then he noted how the Lord commented on the "unsteadiness of the hearts of the children of men," which has so often meant that at the very time when people are being blessed, the softening of their situation causes them to harden their hearts. (Helaman 12:1-2.)

As Alma observed, compulsory humility does have its limitations. (Alma 32:12-15.) Somewhere on the spiritual spectrum between unappreciated blessings and imposed humility lie the obedience and humility that are most healthy and most conducive to growth. In the aforementioned speech, President Lee counseled Latter-day Saint youth to be careful of the trial of "ease and luxury and perhaps too easy ways of learning and education" through which many youth are passing.

We do become "slothful because of the easiness of the

way" (Alma 37:46), just as some are put off by the "simpleness of the way" (1 Nephi 17:41). Significantly, Nephi's warning "Therefore, wo be unto him that is at ease in Zion" (2 Nephi 28:24) follows on the heels (or is in the context) of other specific warnings about how the adversary flatters some away and deceives others by saying there is no hell nor devil, and also about how many will hearken unto the precepts of men, denying the power of God and the gift of the Holy Ghost! Thus ensnared, how could such victims press forward with a love of God and cultivate the gift of the Holy Ghost from whom cometh the fresh word of Christ on which we are to feast?

Ease can be as dangerous as wealth and as risky as power, so far as human development is concerned!

Since we are here to be proved, words of soberness like these from John Taylor are not surprising: "I heard the Prophet Joseph say in speaking to the Twelve on one occasion: 'You will have all kinds of trials to pass through. And it is quite as necessary for you to be tried as it was for Abraham and other men of God, and (he said) God will feel after you, and He will take hold of you and wrench your very heart strings, and if you cannot stand it you will not be fit for an inheritance in the Celestial Kingdom of God.'" (*Journal of Discourses,* 24:197.)

These are hard sayings, but necessary sayings. Since Jesus had to learn obedience by the things which He suffered, can we expect immunity? Immunity from trial and tribulation could also mean, therefore, missing out on essential experiences.

Emulation is the highest and best form of veneration. If we follow the pattern Jesus set and hearken to His counsel, we can be alerted without being depressed by words such as He spoke to His disciples: "These things I have spoken unto you, that in me ye might have peace. In the world ye shall have tribulation: but be of good cheer; I have overcome the world." (John 16:33.) This seeming contradiction between the fact that there would be tribulation in the world and our need to be of good cheer stems from our need to understand that because Jesus has overcome, there will be immortality and resurrection, a perpetuation of personalities beyond death. But more, by his gospel we can have peace within even when there is not peace without. There is no reason, therefore, for us not to be filled with a great sense of hope and to "be of good cheer." The Lord repeated that same urging to His disciples in this dispensation. We can avoid both naive optimism and perpetual pessimism.

There is a higher order of suffering in which even the good pass through tribulation and anguish, which we might characterize as the "trial of the innocent." (Job 9:23.) This is what Peter called "the trial of your faith," and also what he called "the fiery trial." We read how the Prophet Joseph Smith, even though righteous, was sorely tried and was told that what he was passing through would be but "a small moment," and further, that "all these things shall give thee experience, and shall be for thy good." (D&C 122:7.) These are hard sayings but they are true, and they help us understand the suffering of the righteous as distinguished from the suffering we undergo because of our own stupidity and our own sin.

Paul's experience when he came to Macedonia reflects some of the hard realities which are not unique to his time. He mentioned that when he arrived in Macedonia, he was apparently weary; his "flesh had no rest," and he was troubled "on every side, without were fightings, within were fears." Then, bone-weary, he observed, "Nevertheless God, that comforteth those that are cast down, comforted us by the coming of Titus." (2 Corinthians 7:4-6.) Like Paul we can be filled with comfort and be joyful in the midst of tribulation by something as simple as the arrival of a friend. We all need such friends, and even more, to be such a friend!

In modern revelations, the Lord speaks of His people, of having heard their prayers and of accepting their offering, and says, "It is expedient in me that they

should be brought thus far for a trial of their faith."
(D&C 105:19.) We are told elsewhere in the scriptures to
be prepared for tribulation, to be patient in tribulation,
whether in life or in death. We are told that the glory
that follows tribulation cannot be beheld with natural
eyes. (D&C 58:3.) We are told also that "after much
tribulation come the blessings." (D&C 58:4.)

We are even given a vision of an entire church receiving blessings "notwithstanding the tribulation which
shall descend upon you." (D&C 78:14.) Even in the
midst of that tribulation, that church will "stand independent above all other creatures beneath the celestial
world." (D&C 78:14.) The Lord warns us that tribulation can, of course, harden our hearts and cause our
necks to stiffen. (D&C 112:13.) How we cope with tribulation and trial, therefore, is the key.

The Prophet Joseph Smith is a mortal model to contemplate. In an epistle sent to the Saints at Nauvoo, he
disclosed much about himself. He observed that he had
been called upon to pass through many perils in his life,
and that these had been "my common lot all the days of
my life." He observed that "deep water is what I am
wont to swim in." He even observed that such
experiences had almost become "a second nature to me."
Hence he said he shared Paul's feeling of being able to
glory in tribulation.

It is clear in the revelations that we are to cope with
trial and tribulation. There are no special techniques
given to us, no easy ways to cope with it. We are simply
to cope. In the Book of Mormon the persecution upon
members of the church "was a cause of much affliction
to the church; yea, it was the cause of much trial with
the church."

Significantly, in the midst of such pressures, "the
hearts of many were hardened." The prophet further ob-
serves, "Now this was a great trial to those that did stand
fast in the faith; nevertheless, they were steadfast and
immovable in keeping the commandments of God, and
they bore with patience the persecution which was

heaped upon them." (Alma 1:23-25.) Suffering separates the hardy from the frail.

We also read, "Nevertheless the Lord seeth fit to chasten his people; yea, he trieth their patience and their faith." (Mosiah 23:21.) How often our patience is probed and found wanting.

Perhaps the greatest trial to descend upon modern disciples will not be military or political bondage, but environmental bondage in which we are forced to live in a wicked world with evil ever present around us. To rear our children in such circumstances could be a terrible trial. In the military bondage of a whole people there are at least many others who are trying to throw off that bondage. But behavioral bondage (that bondage which causes so many to make allegiance with evil) leaves the minority who cannot condone such a way of life without succor and support from many of their peers, because their peers are part of the problem.

Nor are we promised immediate deliverance. Alma observed in writing to his son Helaman, "For I do know that whosoever shall put their trust in God shall be supported in their trials, and their troubles, and their afflictions, and shall be lifted up at the last day." (Alma 36:3.) Some deliverances simply won't come until we are "lifted up at the last day."

No wonder in such circumstances we read of such imagery as this: "And it came to pass that while he was journeying thither, being weighed down with sorrow, wading through much tribulation and anguish of soul, because of the wickedness of the people who were in the city, . . . it came to pass while Alma was thus weighed down with sorrow, behold an angel of the Lord appeared unto him." (Alma 8:14.)

Thus we are told to trust and to be patient in the midst of such tribulations. The tribulations imposed upon us, often through no fault of our own, are part of the experience of life. There are other tribulations, of course, that come from our own sins and stupidity. That kind of tribulation can be relieved by following the rules of repentance and coming to know the miracle of forgiveness.

Sometimes we are tried by becoming offended. It was Jesus who said that given the nature of the human condition, "it must needs be that offences come; but woe to that man by whom the offence cometh!" (Matthew 18:7.) We are not, therefore, to excuse ourselves because we have been offended. Surely we are to avoid giving offense, but, nevertheless, we are to expect that the nature of life is such that offenses will come.

Perhaps we are not yet ready, as was Mormon, to conclude thusly: "And thus we see that except the Lord doth chasten his people with many afflictions, yea, except he doth visit them with death and with terror, and with famine and with all manner of pestilence, they will not remember him." (Helaman 12:3.) We need to remember, however, that people whose hearts are hardened will have to experience something sufficiently strong to break their hearts and bring them to their senses. If it is true (as it is) that the Lord chasteneth those whom He loves, we would not really want immunity from the chastening of either circumstance or other things.

Because God loves us, He will do what is necessary in order to teach us what we need to know. "Verily, thus saith the Lord unto you whom I love, and whom I love I also chasten that their sins may be forgiven, for with the chastisement I prepare a way for their deliverance in all things out of temptation, and I have loved you." (D&C 95:1.)

In further modern revelation, the Lord says, "Therefore, they must needs be chastened and tried, even as Abraham, who was commanded to offer up his only son. For all those who will not endure chastening, but deny me, cannot be sanctified." (D&C 101:4-5.)

If, as the Lord says in another revelation, His church must become like an army that is "very great," a reference to the fact that the Church must grow numerically, and if, as that same revelation says, His people or church must become sanctified (D&C 105), then we must assume that such sanctification does not occur in the absence of some chastening. For surely some of us are like those whom the Lord described in the revelation: "In the day of their peace they esteemed lightly my counsel; but, in the day of their trouble, of necessity they feel after me." (D&C 101:8.)

A basic purpose of chastening is to learn obedience. "And my people must needs be chastened until they learn obedience, if it must needs be, by the things which they suffer." (D&C 105:6.) We learn obedience by being obedient. In a revelation given through Brigham Young in 1847 we read, "My people must be tried in all things, that they may be prepared to receive the glory that I have for them, even the glory of Zion; and he that will not bear chastisement is not worthy of my kingdom." (D&C 136:31.)

More hard doctrines! But they are given to us that we might know, obey, and endure.

We are told not to despise or resent, therefore, the chastening of the Lord. Paul said, "My son, despise not thou the chastening of the Lord, nor faint when thou art rebuked of him." (Hebrews 12:5.) He further observed, "Now no chastening for the present seemeth to be joyous, but grievous: nevertheless afterward it yieldeth the peaceable fruit of righteousness unto them which are exercised thereby." (Hebrews 12:11.) No wonder we must have eternal perspective to endure chastening, because there would seem to be little pleasure or joy in it and sometimes virtually no immediate understanding of why. But later! Later! For we so often get our witness only after the trial of our faith. (See Ether 12:6.)

It was a marvelous Job who said, "Surely it is meet to be said unto God, I have borne chastisement, I will not offend any more: That which I see not teach thou me; if I have done iniquity, I will do no more." (Job 34:31-32.)

Paul, in writing to the saints in Thessalonica in a very sensitive, sweet epistle, wanted to comfort them "that no man should be moved by these afflictions: for yourselves know that we are appointed thereunto. For verily, when we were with you, we told you before that we should suffer tribulation; even as it came to pass, and ye know." (1 Thessalonians 3:3-4.)

We must even be prepared for the irony that there are those who will enjoy our affliction. Pahoran said this to his friend Moroni: "But behold, there are those who do joy in your afflictions. . . ." (Alma 61:3.)

We can, if we are obedient, be gentled by afflictions; we can be tamed by afflictions; we can be softened by afflictions; we can be consoled in the midst of afflictions; we can be humbled by them. Lehi consoled his son Jacob with this interesting insight: ". . . thou knowest the greatness of God; and he shall consecrate thine afflictions for thy gain." (2 Nephi 2:2.)

We must be obedient to the Lord's timing, too, for the timing of God is not man's timing. In section 101 of the Doctrine and Covenants, the Lord says that in an appointed time, He will pour out His wrath without measure on the earth. It won't be when we think God should come down and rescue us and put an end to it all. It will be when He thinks so. Timing requires us to have a high level of trust, when mere logic and reason are not enough for us to understand. We will simply have to trust and to be obedient.

It is significant in this regard that the Lord's people anciently had to trust Elijah against what probably seemed to some of them to be their own better judgment. In the episode to follow, Elijah seemingly compounded the crunch when there was no obvious reason:

"And Elijah said unto all the people, Come near unto me. And all the people came near unto him. And he repaired the altar of the Lord that was broken down.

"And Elijah took twelve stones, according to the number of the tribes of the sons of Jacob, unto whom the word of the Lord came, saying, Israel shall be thy name:

"And with the stones he built an altar in the name of the Lord; and he made a trench about the altar, as great as would contain two measures of seed.

"And he put the wood in order, and cut the bullock in pieces, and laid him on the wood, and said, Fill four barrels with water, and pour it on the burnt sacrifice, and on the wood.

"And he said, Do it the second time. And they did it the second time. And he said, Do it the third time. And they did it the third time.

"And the water ran round about the altar; and he filled the trench also with water.

"And it came to pass at the time of the offering of the evening sacrifice, that Elijah the prophet came near, and said, Lord God of Abraham, Isaac, and of Israel, let it be known this day that thou art God in Israel, and that I am thy servant, *and that I have done all these things at thy word.*

"Hear me, O Lord, hear me, that this people may know that thou art the Lord God, and that thou hast turned their heart back again.

"Then the fire of the Lord fell, and consumed the burnt sacrifice, and the wood, and the stones, and the dust, and licked up the water that was in the trench." (1 Kings 18:30-38. Italics added.)

Elijah was specifically commanded by God to do just what he did; that is, to pour water on the burnt offering. Elijah was mature and faithful enough to be obedient. We do not know how all of the onlookers felt, yet the collision with the pagans was difficult enough *without* Elijah pouring water on the sacrifice, on the wood, and filling up the trench also with water.

The compounded crunch is a special challenge to our obedience, for it gives us pause and pain. If we are not careful, it can shake us and truly try our faith. Thus obedience isn't something that is merely desirable to take with us in the journey along the straight and narrow—it is as crucial as water itself.

Chapter Four

ON BEING STEADFAST AND HAVING A BRIGHTNESS OF HOPE

The homogenizing of our hopes
can cause a crippling moodiness and
an unnecessary faltering in our steadfastness.
There is a vital distinction between
hopefulness for transitory things and
hopefulness for eternal things.
Hoping for one's pay to be raised, on one
hand, and hoping to be raised from the grave,
on the other, are very different in two ways:
the one hope is transitory, the other eternal;
the hope for a pay raise may be dashed by
men and circumstance, but the hope
for a resurrection is a hope
for that which is already guaranteed.
Here-and-now hopes that go unrealized
must not undercut the ultimate
optimism of the gospel truths.
A loving mother will hope for the return one
day of her runaway son, but the runaway
may elect to stay away; however, he cannot
run far enough to be beyond the redemptive
reach of his Elder Brother!
Therefore, all that is finally worth hoping for
and being steadfast about is bound up in the
future which has been prepared for us by
Jesus of Nazareth. Thus, when we press
forward, it must be "with a
steadfastness in Christ."

Count Leo Tolstoy reportedly said that great prospects lay ahead if Mormonism could succeed in transmitting its unique values forward in time, unmodified. Not losing behavioral uniqueness or theological thrust is a challenge, both for the institution of the Church and for the individuals in it, but never more so than now, when those restored values are in the path of the killer tides in various cultures. Indeed, the surf has already begun to pound! We will need to be very steadfast and to let the brightness of our hope light up a darkened world.

As wave after worldly wave breaks over the rising generation in the Church, there will be casualties. Some waves will be huge, one-time waves; others will be repeater waves, striking again and again. Drugs, pornography, promiscuity, alcoholism, homosexuality, ersatz emancipation movements, divorce, and statism (in which citizens surrender to the state, saying "save us from ourselves") are among such waves.

The skills for survival include a certain buoyancy as these waves heave themselves well beyond their bounds, beyond the traditional impact areas.

No wonder men's hearts will be in commotion with such tossing and tumbling. No wonder we must be especially concerned with effectiveness in the home as well as in the Church. No wonder we must, to use Nephi's words, be filled with "a perfect brightness of hope." Anything less would be too dim in a churning and despairing world.

Will despair deepen in the world? Yes, because "despair cometh because of iniquity" (Moroni 10:22), and therefore, as iniquity increases, so will despair. When discouragement moves us to sin, sin then moves us to despair. But this self-reinforcing tide can be broken only by hope.

If there is no reason to be good, why bother? If there are no absolute rights, there are no real wrongs. And so the unwinding of self and social discipline goes, when hope gives way.

Though battered, tough hope will still trudge out to

call attention to the new season, the new day, the new chance. Faith, we should recall, "is the substance of things *hoped for*." (Hebrews 11:1. Italics added.) Hope is like the infantry's point man on a reconnaissance mission who presses on undaunted as the man of La Mancha.

Indeed the first trait Nephi mentions as being necessary for the journey, when he defines what pressing forward entails, is "a perfect brightness of hope"; then come loving, studying, and enduring. Souls can be summoned by hope, rallied by its "reveille" when no other music can yet be heard. Other sweet sounds will come to stir us, to sustain us, to move us, but that soul scout, hope, is the first friend beckoning on the horizon.

Nor is this hope of which Nephi writes a generalized hope. It is a specific hope that is Christ-centered, including "hope of a glorious resurrection." (D&C 42:45.) We do not fully understand the ecology of faith, hope, and charity, but their interconnectedness is noted time and time again in the scriptures. Moroni speaks of the need for "a more excellent hope" if we are to pursue a more excellent way. (Ether 12:32.)

One of the greatest sources of hope is the Comforter, for He can keep us at our lonely posts when it appears that our comrades have been routed or have deserted. The salvation that secularists preach simply will not be able to generate the hope needed.

Real hope will not exist apart from tribulation, for as Paul said, " . . . tribulation worketh patience; And patience, experience; and experience, hope." (Romans 5:3-4.)

One of the real challenges to hopeful discipleship is our own moodiness and our own moments of discouragement as well as the moods of others. Because moods and discouragement come from so many sources, no chapter (nor indeed a whole book) could deal definitively with this challenge. But some observations might be helpful.

It was Thomas Mann who said, "Time cools, time clarifies; no mood can be maintained quite unaltered through the hours." (*The Magic Mountain.*) Our moods do change, so we need to distinguish between a mood and a basic belief. The Book of Mormon doesn't become untrue because we have had a bad day! When one is down "forty-love," his basic self-esteem should not hinge on achieving a service break! Our moods so often stem from our being disappointed with ourselves or with others. So often the passage of time and/or nightfall tends to exaggerate a disagreement or a disappointment. We are usually much better at dealing with moods well before bedtime, just as inspiration often comes in the morning.

Dark moods can occur when we have been provoked to anger. As Paul said, "Fathers, provoke not your children to anger, lest they be discouraged." (Colossians 3:21.) When we have been provoked to anger, we are often discouraged. Perhaps we are disappointed with a person who has provoked us, but almost always we are disappointed with ourselves.

People who are deeply devoted have high expectations and, if they are not careful, are apt to be victimized by moods more than are those who don't care much about anything or someone who is permanently pessimistic.

Because of gospel truth, we realize that what we do and what other people do really does matter, not only today, but a thousand years from now. If nothing mattered, if nothing in life were wrong, there wouldn't be much to be upset about except existence itself. It's our very awareness of the presence of divine standards that makes the moments matter. Indeed, the interplay of human emotions produces paradoxes. It was William Wordsworth who observed, "In that sweet mood when pleasant thoughts / Bring sad thoughts to the mind." Why that should occasionally be so, we do not fully know, but we do know that sadness is almost always sweetened by enlarged service and increased study.

While some of our worries are immediate and justified, which may account for some of our moods of discouragement, so many of us worry about things that never happen. Emerson observed, "Some of your hurts you have cured, / And the sharpest you still have survived, / But what torments of grief you have endured / From evil which never arrived!"

The disciple should be anxiously engaged and watchful, but he need not be filled with overanxiety to the point of lessened effectiveness. When conscientiousness has caused us to do all that can reasonably be done, then we can, in some serenity, both stand and withstand. Overanxiety, by contrast, is like pulling up the daisies to see how the roots are doing, checking up on the sentries so incessantly that they become trigger-happy, and wringing one's hands instead of folding them in prayer.

Anxiety spreads, and even if our personal "wiring" can stand the voltage from our overanxiety, someone else may blow a fuse because of an overload to which we have contributed.

Sometimes we would be better to express, if we must, our disappointment briefly and then pass on to the next task rather than to sulk. Some athletes who make a poor shot in tennis, for instance, can scold themselves verbally or inwardly and then forget it and go on to the next rally, while other tennis players sulk and sink ever more deeply into mediocre performance.

We may not know how to account for our moods at times, but the fact that these moods pass through us ought not to destabilize us so far as the deep doctrines of the Church are concerned. If down moods cannot be driven out at once, we can at least accelerate their transit times.

It is so easy for one person's bad day to become another person's bad day. A spreading electrical power outage ends up affecting everybody, because early on, the discipline required was abandoned in favor of passing the problem along. Emotional electricity is much like the real thing.

In any objective assessment of life, we can always be reassured as to the things that matter most: Immortality is ours through the gift and grace of Jesus Christ; there is a loving, caring Father in heaven; and we will live eternally under His perfect rule. We have such high promises and absolutely no reason for ultimate discouragement. Therefore, proximate pessimism ought not to envelop us. We ought not to be blitzed by our moods.

When our own miseries seem to preoccupy us, there is merit in reflecting on Jesus' sweet comment to His companions on Calvary. In the midst of indescribable suffering, He could still think of others. The Prophet Joseph Smith in Carthage Jail found time and love enough to particularize with helping comments and reassurances to those who actually had less to fear than he did. A wife dying in a hospital found time and empathy enough in her very last hours to urge her returned-mission-president husband to see to it that her nurse's missionary son got a needed overcoat.

Despair about life and about self is a different thing from the transitory moods that may pass over us. The doctrines of the Church can help us to deal with despair, but moodiness seems best dealt with by service and by prayer. Turning inward is a form of looking back, whereas looking out for others requires just that––looking outward.

There is probably a relationship between the sense of despair some feel and the prophecy that says that in the last days "men's hearts shall fail them." (D&C 45:26.) Another clue is in an Old Testament episode that links the failing of the heart to a loss of courage: "and they were afraid"––because of anticipation of what was coming! (Genesis 42:28.) Anticipated anguish can disarm us and cause us to break even before the battle begins.

People who search for a light at the end of a tunnel other than the light of Jesus Christ will not find it. Knowing, however, that His light is eternal, steadfast, unwavering, and constant can see us through the narrowest passages when steadfastness is most apt to slacken.

So much of steadfastness depends upon our hopefulness, especially hopefulness for a better self.

Someday we will see, with amazement and sadness, how little adjustments in our lives can make such big differences. We can see some of these opportunities (though more quickly in others) even now. There is, for instance, the person who is chronically a few minutes late, who freely spends the time of others by keeping them waiting—who could, if he would, do just what he does now, even at the same pace, but just arise or arrive seven minutes earlier, which would make all the difference in a whole day!

There are others who may never know how much more effective they would be in small groups if they would just utter two comments *fewer*. Still others would be much more effective in influencing others if they would simply smile three times *more* each day.

If, when we are particularly fatigued or harassed, we simply said less than usual, it would help. The regrets per utterance increase when we do not filter out fatigue, selfishness, or peevishness. Further, more thinking beforehand about what we really want to say is the best way of insuring that we say what we want to say.

All such small things that go undone result in a poor performance. This is not to say that there are not major things we need to start doing or to stop doing—but most of the adjustments urgently needed are small, though these would produce major differences in outcomes. These small things are errors that keep us from excellence, like the "almost" of Agrippa.

It was George MacDonald who warned us about fondling our failures and also about how essential it is, each day if we can, to break afresh, outside the crust of self. One of the values of the disciple's *not* looking back is that it trims the tendency to rehearse past errors and to rehash past gripes.

How seldom do we equate hungering and thirsting after righteousness with a deep and constant yearning in ourselves to be better in specific ways? Vague feelings about the need to become better leave us uneasy but unimproved.

We can be sure that if our resolves and action steps are postponed, our hunger and the thirst are not yet very great. Whereas a simple, twenty-four-hour fast soon reminds us of the need for food and water, we go for weeks, months, yes, years, without really hungering for a real change in our behavior. Oh, yes, the passive yearning is there all right, but it is not yet real hunger or real thirst! Of course, our attempts at improvement do produce some failures and frustrations, so frequently our frustrations are blessings struggling to be born—the labor pains of progress.

Just how God will use the simple and the weak to acclaim the gospel and to thresh the world by the power of His spirit is not completely clear. But let us make no mistake, there will be some rather dramatic things happen. The Lord said, "The weak things of the world shall come forth and break down the mighty and strong ones, that man should not counsel his fellow man, neither trust in the arm of flesh." (D&C 1:19.) The Lord has said further that He will "call upon the weak things of the world, those who are unlearned and despised, to thrash the nations by the power of [His] Spirit." (D&C 35:13.) To do such things will take steadfastness and hopefulness on our part. It will be no picnic at the park.

Elsewhere the Lord has said that He has given the fullness of His gospel in plainness and simplicity "to prepare the weak for those things which are coming on the earth, and for the Lord's errand in the day when the weak shall confound the wise, and the little ones become a strong nation, and two shall put their tens of thousands to flight." (D&C 133:58.)

One thing is clear: in stressful situations, our deficiencies become more obvious. The Lord has said that He "showeth us our weakness that we may know that it is by his grace, and his great condescensions unto the children of men, that we have power to do these things." (Jacob 4:7.) Additionally, he said, "And if men come unto me I will show unto them their weakness. I give unto men weakness that they may be humble; and my grace is sufficient for all men that humble themselves before me; for if they humble themselves before me, and have faith in me, then will I make *weak things become strong unto them."* (Ether 12:27. Italics added.) Difficulties sometimes put our deficiencies on display; it is then that we must be especially humble if we are to be made strong subsequently.

If the Saints have the Spirit of the Lord with them, they will have the perspective and the necessary steadfastness. Before the end comes, as Jesus promised, "when ye shall hear of wars and commotions, be not terrified: for these things must first come to pass; but the end is not by and by." (Luke 21:9.)

The days will come when, unless we are so equipped, society's scoffing and scolding could make us ashamed for even hoping in the midst of such despair and in the midst of general surrender to sin.

It was William Law, an English clergyman of the eighteenth century, who said, "If it is said the very hairs of your head are all numbered, is it not to teach us that nothing, not the smallest things imaginable, happen to us by chance? But if the smallest things we can conceive are declared to be under the divine direction, need we, or can we, be more plainly taught that the greatest things of life, such as the manner of our coming into the world, our parents, the time, and other circumstances of our birth and condition, are all according to the eternal purposes, direction, and appointment of Divine Providence?" (*A Serious Call to a Devout and Holy Life* [Grand Rapids, Mich.: Sovereign Grace, 1971], p. 148.)

Law also warned that "no people have more occasion to be afraid of the approaches of pride than those who have made some advances in a pious life. For pride can grow as well as our virtues, as our vices, and steals on us on all occasions." (Ibid., p. 99.)

Being steadfast includes relentless resistance to such vices as pride; it also includes resisting the growing indifference to integrity in the world.

The road and path of integrity has infinite intersections each requiring decisions, each requiring the manifestation of our integrity. Integrity is more easily maintained when the tradition of following proper counsel and directions is strong enough within the person that it draws upon the power of habit.

President Joseph F. Smith has called on us to educate our very desires. This is wise counsel, for nothing interrupts steadfastness like catering to our selfish desires.

William Law said, "Now all trouble and uneasiness is founded in the want of something or other; would we therefore know the true cause of our troubles and disquiet, we must find out the cause of our wants; because that which creates, and increases our wants, does in the same degree create, and increase our trouble and disquiets. . . . The man of pride has a thousand wants, which only his pride has created; and these render him as full of trouble, as if God had created him with a thousand appetites, without creating anything that was proper to satisfy them." (Ibid., pp. 57-58.)

Charles Wagner warned, "Let your needs rule you; pamper them, and you will see them multiply like insects in the sun. The more you give them, the more they demand."

The justice of God permits no special deal for disciples. We must subdue our selfishness; we must endure the pain of prioritizing. We must cope with the variables of the second estate. There can be no later outcry by the nonbelievers that they were ultimately deprived of an *equal chance* to believe and to follow. For disciples there is no spiritual equivalent to the "prime rate" or the "most-favored nation" clause. Blessings come the same way to all—by obedience to the laws on which these blessings are predicated, and in no other way. (D&C 130:20.)

The disciple must, therefore, be careful about confusing announcements of intentions with accomplishments as far as his progress on the path is concerned.

Are spiritual highs followed by bad days? Indeed. The day of Pentecost, a historical high, was apparently followed shortly thereafter by circumstances in which some members of the Church of Christ began to hedge as far as living the law of consecration was concerned. Because, as far as people are concerned, the gospel net "gathereth of every kind," we must assume that such variety will produce disappointment. The critics of the Church, who are often those within the Church, frequently say, "Why doesn't the Church do this or that?" or "Why does the Church do this or that?" Those who desire to make the greatest demands of the Church are usually those who make the fewest demands of themselves in terms of *their* discipleship.

There is another clue to maintaining our steadfastness: We should judge the warnings given to us by their accuracy and relevancy, not by the finesse or the diplomacy by which the warnings are given. The disciple's commitment to truth must be to truth, without an inordinate concern for the method of delivery. Of course, it takes real humility to listen under some circumstances. The Paul Reveres in our lives may have voices too shrill, use bad grammar, ride a poor horse, and may pick the oddest hours to warn us. But the test of warnings is their accuracy, not their diplomacy.

President Ezra Taft Benson, a careful watcher of events, maintains a certain buoyancy and cheerfulness we would do well to watch. Such buoyancy comes not from ignoring enveloping events, but from noticing these and yet looking beyond them to promises having to do with how the kingdom will finally prevail. In a conference address he suggested at least a dozen ways to lift our spirits: repentance, prayer, service, work, health, reading, blessing, fasting, friends, music, endurance, and the setting of short-term and long-range goals. (*Conference Report*, October 1974, pp. 91-94.) These practical reminders are, in fact, the very sort of things we need to do in order to maintain our discipleship in the midst of varied challenges.

President David O. McKay said that "it is our duty to seek to acquire the art of being cheerful," since a cheerful spirit "will hold in check the demons of despair and stifle the power of discouragement and hopelessness." (*Treasures of Life* [Deseret Book, 1965], p. 60.)

President McKay also advocated striving "to make somebody else happy and see how quickly your own soul is filled with joy." (Ibid., p. 372.) He urged us to make specific attempts even for a few days at a time to see how moodiness could be dispelled. Pressing forward implies initiation, acting for ourselves righteously rather than waiting for life to act upon us.

Then, speaking of larger considerations, he reminded us that "the Church of Christ is established never more to be thrown down or given to another people" and how "conditions were never more favorable or promising in the Church than today." (Ibid., p. 465.) In that respect, events and developments of recent years should give us even greater reasons to be filled with hope and to be of good cheer.

President McKay's wise counselor of so many years, President J. Reuben Clark, Jr., once paid special tribute to a particular group of pioneers in an essay titled "To Them of the Last Wagon," praising those who traveled in the dust of other pioneers, who did not get the first view of the next horizon, who had done their less glamorous duties, and who had pressed forward anyway. Sometimes in the Church we forget that there are modern equivalents of those steadfast and hopeful souls in the last wagon.

Thus, maintaining discipleship requires just what Nephi stipulated in order to press forward. We should be grateful for the brightness of hope that we have. This perfect brightness of hope is in stark contrast to the dull, gray, and cloud-covered sky of secularism. In the latter there are no sunrises or sunsets because there is no *Son!* It is by the bright light of Christ that we can better see everybody and everything else and thereby be filled with justified hope.

When one sums up the most common causes of a failure to press forward with discipleship, these causes are impressive but clearly not unassailable. Removing such roadblocks on the straight and narrow way is actually attainable, especially if tackled one or two at a time. The blocks include the following:

1. Mistaking the entrance gate for the main gate and hence pausing because all seems to be done. This silly situation can be quite an effective roadblock, because *before* we went through the entrance gate there were no illusions about our having arrived. Now such illusions can be disabling.

2. Strolling casually forward instead of pressing forward, in which one gets the sensation of motion and direction but without perspiration. This is a very effective deterrent to discipleship.

3. Moving forward with spurts of pressing followed by prolonged periods of pausing. This is much like strolling, except it provides the sensation of speed at least occasionally for those who like it.

4. Going on sidetrips and diversions that appeal to one's sense of fair play to oneself, for, after all, we are *entitled* to some respites from rigorousness. This leads to some AWOLs, but also, more regrettably, to some desertions.

5. Being overcome by the cares of the world, which we are very much still in. The world can soak up our time and talents in some worthy but not crucial causes, especially if Christ slips from the center of our lives. One thing seems clear: Unless we live so that we are not "of" the world, the probability of being overcome by the cares of the world is very great.

6. Seeking and listening to the praise of the world. At first this seems less dangerous than getting entangled with the things of the world. The problem arises when the praise of the world deflects us from removing the deficiencies in our discipleship.

7. Being discouraged and moody, which are hard on hope and fatal for the precious perspective we need in order to survive spiritually.

8. Being too much with the world, whose values and

life-styles end up draining off our devotion and diminishing our faith. Discipleship is not and cannot be monastic, nor can we be like the one-time detached Jonah. But we can reduce our vulnerabilities if we practice affirmative associational patterns. Sometimes, as with Lot, breaking away is the only wise response. One wonders, by the way, if when Judas Iscariot went to the chief priests, that was his *first* conversation with any of them.

9. Relying on defective hope, which is like using a parachute that works most of the time. Hopes not grounded in the gospel are too much at the mercy of men and circumstance.

10. Being frozen in self-pity or serving others without love. Both of these problems grow out of inadequate love of God and, therefore, men. There is a terrible, self-reinforcing cycle here: When we love too little, we serve others less and less, and serving them less and less, we love them less and less.

11. Failing to feast upon the words of Christ regularly. We are fasting rather than feasting; what a difference an "e" makes!

12. Faltering and grumbling rather than enduring. Ironically, this may be more of a challenge as life goes on. Life's final exams may be more difficult than midterms and comprehensive exams are, and more taxing than routine quizzes. The fine young man who came to Jesus asking what he must yet do was not the only individual who will be asked to make just one more sacrifice or to face just one more test before the end.

13. Refusing to give up one's special sins. Sometimes we cling to these as if they were (of all things) "security blankets"! C. S. Lewis described the dynamic: "But the time comes on when, though the pleasure becomes less and less and the craving fiercer and fiercer, and though he knows that joy can never come that way, yet he prefers to joy the mere fondling of unappeasable lust and would not have it taken from him. . . . even when he can scratch no more he'd rather itch than not." (*The Great*

Divorce [New York: Macmillan, 1974], p. 70.)

There are, to be sure, other and equal obstacles in the path. En masse they are more impressive than when examined carefully and individually. There is at least one remedy for each, a remedy well within reach. And there are always mortal helpers to help move the road-blocks. Even if we can do no more than sincerely desire to remove these roadblocks, we must let that desire really work in us without trying to repress or stifle it. (See Alma 32:2.) Strength can be summoned as that desire grows. Just as we are promised that we will not be tempted above that which we are able to endure (see 1 Corinthians 10:13; D&C 64:20), likewise no roadblock confronts us that cannot be removed!

Being confused about the two gates—repentance and baptism by water and fire, the first gate, and the end of the straight and narrow trail, the second and final gate—can be cleared up by reading the scriptures and feasting upon the words of Christ. One cannot read very far in the scriptures without realizing how much God has concentrated on giving us guidance for the journey between the two gates.

There is no such thing as a casual Christian. Conscience can help us, as can feasting upon the word of Christ. So can being around those who are serious—not strolling—disciples, for their commitment is contagious. Affirmative associations are vital in this regard. The best way to become anxiously engaged is to become engaged fully in the work; then the need for it becomes not only obvious, but is self-reinforced. Every program as well as every principle of the Church carries within itself its own witness that it is true.

Spurts followed by slackness are remedied by developing our love of God and man, since people's needs do not take a recess. We are always surrounded by more opportunities for service than we utilize. There is a sobering corollary to the scriptural example, "When gave I thee to drink" (see Matthew 25:37), and that corollary is the query "When did I refuse thee drink?"

Then will the evidence be presented as to how many times we passed people in need and "noticed them not." Besides, measured steadiness is more efficient than spurts and then a slackening. Further, we are less apt to "wear away" in prudent persistence than in a combination of breathlessness and ease. Sometimes we may reward our breathlessness with a respite that turns into a permanent repose; we do this by reflecting on all that we have done up to now and how it is surely now someone else's turn.

Sidetrips and scenic views can be responded to much as suggested above, but with this added comment: enduring suggests a persistent pace forward. When we put our hand to the plow, peripheral vision is helpful, but it is turning the head that diverts our gaze and cuts into our concentration––all of which makes faulty furrows. To go on a "sabbatical" sidetrip is to use additional energy and talent that are more needed elsewhere. Thus renewal, repose, and reflection in the "sabbaths" along the trail are needed, but if we misuse those "sabbaths," then we have broken also our stride and the momentum necessary for pressing forward.

One way of putting the cares of the world (some of which are worth caring about) in their proper place is to ask ourselves such simple questions as, "If I knew I had only six months to live, what small handful of things would I most want to get done?" Or, "How many of my present cares are actually connected with things that will persist beyond the grave?" Answering such questions honestly can be quite helpful. But the thing that is most helpful is to have quality cares that will crowd out the cares of the world. Such can occur if we know that immortality is coming, that our accountability is real, that God really is our Father, and that men and women are actually our brothers and sisters. Such realizations grow only when we are serving God and man.

Our experiences in so serving, loving, and learning are enhanced immeasurably by study of the scriptures, which give us a longitudinal look at God and man. No one's circle of concern has ever been shrunken by studying the scriptures, nor do the cares of the world grow in such a climate. Further, the unblinking, unvarnished reminders in the scriptures about the shortness of this life and the inevitability of the judgment can bring the cold chill that is sometimes necessary to stimulate the mind and the heart. Tell a dishonest banker that the auditors have arrived unannounced and you'll get his mind off his golf score!

The praise of the world can be put in perspective by the scriptures. Much of the praise of the world is true and is sincerely given, though phony praise abounds. Feedback from family and from the institution of the Church can give much-needed perspective. A friend, upon being elected president of a state senate, told his wife of this honor with some satisfaction, whereupon his wife said, "That's nice, but please take out the garbage!"

The point is not to counter the deserved praise of the world with unappreciation, but rather that we must not retire into our vault and count the coins of commendation. The rule should be humble appreciation for deserved praise, but not to savor praise. The temptation to loiter is sometimes greatest at the end of the spiritual feasts following the last hymn, the last handshake, and the last amen. We must move on. We do not read that the Lord lingered after the Last Supper.

Cuddling compliments is as dangerous as fondling failures, for neither gives us a true picture of ourselves. Apparently, the Prophet Joseph needed the perspective that came from hearing himself compared to Job—and then Jesus! (D&C 121.) The crosses on the shoulders of our fellow travelers may not always be visible, but they are there. Friendship and Christian conversation can help. Part of enduring consists of deflecting not only bad thoughts but bad moods, and the "no vacancy" sign is still the best way to turn them away. A life filled with service and outgoing concern leaves little room for more than fleeting disquietude. One cannot read of Job (or an earlier Joseph) and, seeing how they coped, really ask God, "What have you done for me lately?"

75

One can fellowship and friendship others—indeed we must—without taking out a membership in the country club at Sodom. There may be times when we must speak out sharply as did the Prophet Joseph in Carthage when foul conversation had been endured. There are still other times when silence is the strongest rebuke. Mostly, however, we need to summon up sweetness, not indignation, and to respond firmly but softly, if necessary. One of the great advantages of the kingdom is fellowship, and we need to receive as much as to give. Sufficient unto the day, for most of us, are the entanglements of the world—without enlarging upon these. Public relations points can be made for the kingdom in varied circumstances, but to plan proper settings for association with the nonbeliever can be as vital as the substance of what is said while in such associations.

A helping grace with regard to hope is to sort out more clearly our ultimate hopes and the clear reassurances that we have been given concerning these larger things from the human aspiration of a proximate nature. By letting our hopes tumble together indiscriminately, we diminish and confuse them. Just as a bad day does not render the Book of Mormon invalid, neither can an unrealized hope for a more fair and sensitive Scoutmaster in one's ward (to help a shy son) hold hostage our guaranteed hope for justice when we are before the judgment bar of God.

Being a mechanical Mormon is best avoided by increased service *plus* prayers for patience and persistence *plus* a correct understanding of how we were actually given assignments in the premortal world that we must now take seriously. Further, as Moroni tells us, we cannot enter the celestial kingdom unless we have charity. (Ether 12:34.) Self-pity shrinks us, but we become larger by enlarged service and extended concern for others. It is not wise to compare crosses, but association at least permits us to see crosses that appear to be much larger and heavier than our own. Seeing such can stimulate our steadfastness and our gratitude.

76

In a study group the lesson giver asked each participant to write down what his major problem was. Then he showed a film of a gallant lady, born without arms, who has done remarkably well in taking life steadfastly in stride and without self-pity or murmuring. After the film, the instructor simply said, "Now would any of you like to tell of your major problem?"

Sometimes when we disappointedly describe our personal experiences, we speak of having gone two steps forward and one back, and surely this is sometimes true. Perhaps, however, we may mean something else without realizing it. Sometimes we move several steps forward and are so startled at how far we have come that, finding it too good to be true, we fall back without cause. There has been no encounter with the enemy—just with a startled self. The enemy withdrew days, even weeks, ago. It happens in all wars, including the war with the former self, except there are no tactically timid generals to blame, just a shy self grown too accustomed to a line of resistance that is no longer there. Nor do such gains mean that the adversary has ordered a general retreat—just that there is more territory for the taking than we imagine because we are too unhopeful and too reluctant to reconnoiter steadfastly.

Thus, being steadfast is focused faith at work, featuring service that springs from serenity, not uncertainty. Deeds done by disciples are not performed merely to dissolve doubt through busyness, but out of a strong but quiet assurance that says that not only can good individuals actually make needed differences, but that they must!

Finally, there is a subtle source of strength upon which we can draw to add to our steadfastness. While quietly counting our blessings, we can remember these blessings were given to us by God *because* we obeyed the very laws upon which they were predicated. Thus, if we now do once more what we have done before—obey steadfastly—God will do again what He did once before: bless!

77

Chapter Five

ON PREPARING A GENERATION OF DESTINY

Occasionally some one arises
who feels that it is his duty to inform the
world that the old members of the Church
are still faithful, . . . but that the rising
generation is departing. . . . I am here to
testify that this is not true. There may be . . .
those among us who are not faithful, who do
turn from the footsteps of their fathers . . . ,
but so far as the Latter-day Saints are
concerned, the majority of them will not turn
from the faith of their fathers.
(Joseph Fielding Smith, *Conference Report,*
April 1925, p. 74.)
Oh, youth and young adults
of the Church, remember the Son of God is
your best friend, and His light is ever shining.
In some ways, His light is like that of the sun;
we may turn away from the light,
but it is still there; its rays and warmth only
seem to be gone because of our moodiness
and the cloud cover of our concerns.
Likewise, Christ is ever
there. We may ignore Him, but He will break
through, for our provincialism will not keep
His love from shining upon us.

The theme for this chapter has been chosen neither to flatter nor to frighten the youth and young adults of the Church; rather, to inform and hopefully to inspire them. None of the rising generation has been placed on this planet by chance or for random reasons. This is their appointed time, and they come to this age talent-laden and perhaps even with a little anxiety and perplexity as the drama of these days unfolds about them. Therefore, this chapter is addressed to our youth and young adults.

You will see both wonderful and awful things. Many of you will see and experience such things as these:

1. Because the days preceding the second coming of Jesus will, in some respects, be like the days of Noah, there will be in your time, as then, much violence and corruption. (Moses 8:28; Genesis 6:11.) We deplore but cannot ignore the gathering storm, but you should not be dismayed by the darkness.

2. The love of many will wax cold. Indifference, insensitivity, and cruelty will extend beyond obvious manifestations, such as abortion, to other things as well. Previous societies in deep decay and deterioration were characterized by the words *past feeling, without order,* and *without mercy.* (See Moroni 9:18.)

3. Many so-called Christians will end up denying, as Peter prophesied, "the Lord that bought them." (2 Peter 2:1.) Denying the divinity of Jesus will be accompanied by denials of the reality of Lucifer. Equivocating ecclesiastics will play to the galleries because many of their constituents "will not endure sound doctrine . . . and shall be turned unto fables." (2 Timothy 4:3-4.) Many nonbelievers will follow such popular leaders, and it will be by such followers that "the way of truth shall be evil spoken of." (2 Peter 2:2.)

No attacks on the Church will be more bitter or more persistent than those made in the Salt Lake Valley. No taunts will be more shrill than those of apostates and excommunicants. In that valley and in the state of Utah,

Church members will be accused of the "crime" of being a majority! Some clever defectors will imitate their model, Satan, and will try to take others over the side with them. Elsewhere, you will encounter the same sort of snobbery that gave rise to "can any good thing come out of Nazareth?"

4. These will be times of "unnatural affection," which unnaturalness will seek to become the norm. You will see shades of Sodom and glimpses of Gomorrah. You will see firsthand the growth of teachings similar to those which misled men and women in the Book of Mormon who sought to fashion a standardless society in which "whatsoever a man did was no crime." (Alma 30:17.)

5. Just as all the prophecies heralding Christ's first advent were fulfilled, so will be all the prophecies heralding His second coming. Some of them may puzzle us, but increasingly it is possible to see through "glass, darkly" (1 Corinthians 13:12) how such prophecies might come to pass, such as the one which implies that some will one day say that Christ will come again, but in the form of a woman. (D&C 49:22.) Both false Christs and antichrists will be present. Satan's smorgasbord will be as varied as it is poisonous.

The daughters of Zion, no less than the bearers of the priesthood, are a parallel part of the youth of the Church of whom President Joseph Fielding Smith said that a majority would remain faithful. The daughters of the world may grow more shrill, more hard, more selfish, and less motherly—but the faithful daughters of Zion will be ladies of light; they will be elect because they have elected to follow in the footsteps of the faithful women of God who have existed in all dispensations of time. That we know less than we would like of these marvelous women of God should fill us with anticipation for the day when there will be a fullness of their record before us, a part of all that God will yet reveal.

Service less reported is service still. Contributions are never really measured in column inches of coverage in newspapers or even in the scriptures. Indeed, their deferred recognition only mirrors faintly the quiet queenliness of One we shall meet and greet when we leave "this frail existence."

We must not be dismayed if the adversary strikes at the family through divorce and also through fomenting lives of desperation, or when he encourages people to drop their loyalty to the Prophet, or when he strikes at chastity through creating disarray along the path of procreation. All of these things strike at the plan of salvation against which the adversary and his followers once revolted.

President George Albert Smith observed that the adversary knows "that his end is drawing near." Thus, we can expect him to expend himself in final fury against the work of God and goodness everywhere. President George Q. Cannon told us that "for generations there has been an indifference manifested by the adversary of truth to the systems of religion which have prevailed among men. When men partake of error, . . . then there is indifference manifested by the adversary; . . . religious movements are regarded by him with unconcern. . . . But the moment the Holy Priesthood of God is restored, . . . then all hell is moved. . . ." (*Journal of Discourses* 11:227.) Now that the Church of Jesus Christ is growing and prospering spiritually, "all hell is moved."

Recall how a young Joseph Smith was puzzled as to why he, in his youth and obscurity and poverty, "should be thought a character of sufficient importance to attract the attention of the great ones of the most popular sects of the day, and in a manner to create in them a spirit of the most bitter persecution and reviling." (Joseph Smith 2:23.) Well, so it is (and will be) with us, collectively, especially as the Church is brought forth out of obscurity. If the Church were not true, our enemies would be bored rather than threatened, and acquiescent rather than anxious. Hell is moved only when things move heavenward.

President Brigham Young noted early in his Church

experience that it was revealed to him that as the Church extended and expanded into the nations of the world (which is now happening with unparalleled momentum), so in like manner and simultaneously would the power of the adversary rise. It is a cheek-by-jowl and wheat-by-tares picture that is emerging.

Note such happy hallmarks such as these:

1. You have already lived to see the prophesied gathering to the Holy Land at least partially fulfilled. Much more will yet happen there. It is a land with a dramatic past and a very dramatic future.

2. You will see the Church, the "army" of the Lord, "become very great." (D&C 105:31.) Numerically how many is that? We only know that it is more than our present size. However, we must be ever humble, remembering as Moses told ancient Israel, "The Lord did not set his love upon you, nor choose you, because ye were more in number than any people; for ye were the fewest of all people." (Deuteronomy 7:7.) They, then, and we, now, are His covenant people with His work to do––for the sake of all mankind!

3. You will see the gospel preached in every nation "for a witness" but not always in the traditional ways.

4. You will help to establish, among all who will, the Lord's righteousness in a time when men will be "going about to establish their own righteousness" (Romans 10:3), according to "the fashion of this world."

5. You will help to provide the example of fine family life in a time when many families are disintegrating.

6. Being faithful, you will be able to help to prepare Zion for the time seen by President John Taylor, who prophesied:

"Those who will not take up their sword to fight against their neighbor must needs flee to Zion for safety. And they will come, saying, we do not know anything of the principles of your religion, but we perceive that you are an honest community; you administer justice and righteousness, and we want to live with you and receive

82

the protection of your laws, but as for your religion we will talk about that some other time. Will we protect such people? Yes, all honorable men.

"When the people shall have torn to shreds the Constitution of the United States the Elders of Israel will be found holding it up to the nations of the earth and proclaiming liberty and equal rights to all men, and extending the hand of fellowship to the oppressed of all nations. This is part of the programme, and as long as we do what is right and fear God, he will help us and stand by us under all circumstances." (*Journal of Discourses* 21:8.)

In such dramatic circumstances you will need those virtues which President George Q. Cannon ascribed to those of the latter days: courage, determination, and "obedience to God under all circumstances." (*Journal of Discourses* 11:230.) You will be able to do as President Harold B. Lee counseled and not place a question mark where the Lord has placed a period.

The holders of God's priesthood who are faithful share in the fellowship of foreordination, being called, Alma said, "according to the foreknowledge of God, on account of their exceeding faith and good works." (Alma 13:3.) You, youth and young adults of the Church, come to this life not only trailing traits and talents from your premortal experience, but you also come having manifested good works in that same earlier experience-- from which there is a carry-over commitment.

You have come to blend capacity and opportunity. You have come to see fulfilled and to help to fulfill certain prophecies. All of you who have been called to holy callings, according to Alma, are called on account of your faith, *here and before.* The special daughters of Zion share in this same unfolding drama, for we can neither succeed without them nor go anywhere in the world to come--anywhere that really matters--without them. Believe, therefore, not only in the promises concerning the Church, but in the promises concerning you, individually.

Believe also in yourselves not only for what you already are, but for what you have the power to become. For inlaid in the unfolding collective drama of the development of Zion are thousands of smaller dramas, bold and breathtaking. Those are the chapters in your books of life yet to be written, but which are known beforehand to our Heavenly Father.

The Church has done many difficult things, and from these achievements one would not wish to detract. But all the easy things the Church has had to do have been done. From now on it is high adventure!

Do not be ashamed of the Lord or His leaders, for as Paul counseled young Timothy: "For God hath not given us the spirit of fear; but of power, and of love, and of a sound mind." (2 Timothy 1:7.) With the Spirit of God, with love, and with sound minds and sound doctrines, you can be discerning disciples.

What a glorious day is yours! Will there be trials and tribulations? Yes, and some on a scale never before seen. (Matthew 24:21.) The Lord said, "And the saints also shall hardly escape; nevertheless, I, the Lord, am with them. . . ." (D&C 63:34.)

While we do not think of it this way very often, the rising generation has some genuine responsibilities to the older generation still living. We are not immune to influence from you. We not only regard you as the seedbearers of a celestial culture to come, but our own journey can be hastened by your pressing forward. About A.D. 3, an emerging generation of Lamanite youth "became for themselves," discounting the influence of their righteous parents, and many young adults "were led away." Then this telling observation about how we always need each other was given: ". . . the Lamanites . . . began to decrease as to their faith and righteousness, because of the wickedness of the rising generation." (3 Nephi 1:29-30.) Lowering standards in the rising generations can create an undertow that affects all ages.

We have seen, in just the past decade, various youth movements wash over shaky adults who gave way under

84

pressure. Some adults, strangely enough, replaced their old values, of all things, with youth worship! The last thing youth needs is to be envied or worshiped.

The Church is a beacon to all mankind, promising a special liberty and deliverance from the environmental bondage of evil, from ignorance concerning the purposes of life, from passing fads, and from the poison of petty selfishness.

The following eloquent lines, which are on a bronze tablet affixed to the welcoming Statue of Liberty, were written by Emma Lazarus, but well they might describe the beckoning that is the gospel of Jesus Christ:

". . . From her beacon hand
Glows world-wide welcome. . . .
. . . Give me your tired, your poor,
Your huddled masses yearning to breathe free,
The wretched refuse of your teeming shore,
Send these, the homeless, tempest-tossed, to me:
I lift my lamp beside the golden door."

Yes, to those weary of the world, tired of sin, emptied of hope by secular odysseys, the Church lifts its lamp beside the golden door of salvation and exaltation.

Your generation of destiny will help to usher through those golden gates the greatest numbers ever in this, and perhaps any, dispensation. Do not fail to keep your personal rendezvous!

Chapter Six

ON KEEPING THE SECOND GREAT COMMANDMENT

And the second is like unto
it, Thou shalt love thy neighbour as thyself.
(Matthew 22:39.)
And now I know that this
love which thou hast had for the children of
men is charity; wherefore, except men
shall have charity they cannot inherit that
place which thou hast prepared
in the mansions of thy Father.
(Ether 12:34.)
It is by loving and not by
being loved that one can come nearest
to the soul of another.
(George MacDonald, *An Anthology*, p. 99.)

It would be too easy to pass off the challenge of the second great commandment by simply assuming that anyone who really keeps the first great commandment can be counted on to keep the second. The assumption would be true but not specifically helpful.

The first commandment is clearly first, not second, but the purpose of focusing on the second is that it is "like unto" the first, and almost all of us find keeping it such a continuing, demanding dimension of discipleship. Unless we can be making measurable progress in relation to the second commandment, in what we do and how we serve, we are apt to experience the joylessness and the sense of harassment that always accompany service without love.

We cannot adequately acknowledge the existence of

our brothers and sisters by merely doffing a doctrinal hat. We have to be genuinely and regularly concerned with their welfare and development. Further, as we serve in the Church, we must remember that the genius of the gospel includes more than merely helping those who are already friends to love each other more. The gospel also helps those who might not naturally like each other to appreciate each other; those who are strangers, even enemies, can become friends. But, as in the case of seeking revelation, we must do more than take thought "save it were to ask" for such an outcome in our lives. (D&C 9:7.)

In living together as saints, we surely feel and see each other's faults, but when we look at each other through the lens of the gospel and by the light of heaven, we also see in others attributes and qualities that we little imagined were there. The gospel does not ask us to close our eyes to any reality; rather it helps us to open our eyes both more widely and more appreciatively.

Pressing forward, therefore, includes pressing forward in building relationships with others—not passivity, not pausing or even trudging along with heart, eyes, and mind partially closed. To travel the pathway in the latter manner is to miss the walking wounded. To press forward with heart and eyes cast down is to be so filled with self-concern and self-pity that we have no time or empathy for those who really do have problems, and we therefore "pass them by and notice them not."

Pressing forward without looking back too much is recommended for the same wise reasons some are told not to look down when climbing lest the heights dizzy them. All of us are acrophobes so far as the ascending straight and narrow is concerned.

Perhaps a reason for not pressing forward in developing our capacity to love is that we have come to think of being responsible for our brothers and sisters in the wrong way.

Cain asked, "Am I my brother's keeper?" (Genesis 4:9.) Presumably he responded to the Lord's inquiry either in sarcasm or defensiveness (or both). Cain's rhetorical question causes many of us to assume automatically that we *are* our brother's keeper. Presumably this happens because we link up the assumed answer to the rhetorical question with the gospel view of mankind in which we are truly brothers and sisters, not, as some say, just stranded mutants on a planet that is a pointless point in space.

First, let us examine the circumstances. Cain was *not* Abel's keeper, but he was his brother. Brother and keeper relationships are very different. The former emphasizes concern, the latter control.

Cain slew Abel and even "glorified in that which he had done," saying: "I am free. . . ." (Moses 5:33.) Cain also coveted Abel's flocks. Thus, we should distinguish between our need for brotherly love and being our brother's keeper. Cain not only failed to love Abel, he didn't even care enough about his relationship with Abel to want to improve their relationship.

Abel had found favor with the Lord and Cain had not. This was Cain's fault, not Abel's. This brief focus on that sad but illuminating event is necessary before moving not to the assumed issue, but to the real challenge: How, specifically, can we do better in keeping the second great commandment?

One of the ways in which we can actively pursue the second great commandment, and thus be better brothers and sisters, is to be willing to work at improving relationships that are in trouble. Most of us have such relationships from time to time. In fact, we have an *obligation* to work out impasses as well as trespasses in interpersonal relationships. The Savior said, "Moreover if thy brother shall trespass against thee, go and tell his fault between thee and him alone: if he shall hear thee, thou hast gained thy brother." (Matthew 18:15.) To take the initiative in repairing or strengthening a relationship takes both love and courage. Others don't always respond to such initiatives; some peacemakers are spurned. Absent such initiatives, however, the impasses remain or deepen.

Still another way of being brotherly is to work on our relationships that are essentially good but that could be even richer; many of these need to be enriched even though these are basically healthy.

Another way of improving the quality of relationships with our brothers and sisters is to ask ourselves, more often than we do, this simple question: "Whose needs am I trying to meet?" If we think of others in terms of the impact of our actions and plans on their needs, this will give us perspective that could deepen and enrich brotherhood. Ego trips are almost always made on someone else's expense account!

Because our view of the brotherhood of man is much more than biological brotherhood, we, as Latter-day Saints, must do more than we do. We should see each other with a special perspective. Higher views call for higher performance.

The precious perspective of the gospel lifts us outside an otherwise finite framework. G. K. Chesterton urged us to enlarge our circles of concern: "How much larger your life would be if your self could become smaller in it; if you could really look at other men with common curiosity and pleasure. . . . You would begin to be interested in them, because they were not interested in you. You would break out of this tiny and tawdry theatre in which your own little plot is always being played, and you would find yourself under a freer sky, in a street full of splendid strangers." (*Orthodoxy* [Garden City, N.Y.: Image Books, 1959], pp. 20-21.)

Our provincialism protrudes even into brotherly concerns, for it is sometimes seen in our prayers—in those fervent feelings sent heavenward at times in which we seek to hasten or to slow down time. We seek the speeding of time because of a loved one's suffering, or to slow time by holding back the dawn because a furlough is soon to end. We forget, being children, that others with opposite needs are in this same dimension of time with us: to hasten time as we wish would be to end someone's final visit with aging parents, or to slacken the speed of time would be to prolong the passing of another stranded in senility lo these many years.

5. The Lord advises us, "Let every man esteem his brother as himself." (D&C 38:24.) There is an inescapable ecology of esteem, an intertwining of interests. If, for instance, we have low self-esteem, we are far less likely to build rich relationships with our Heavenly Father and with our fellowmen. If we have low self-esteem we are far less likely to feel good about life, since we do not feel reasonably good about ourselves. Thus, one of the important and specific ways we can help our brothers and sisters is to help them build deserved self-esteem. We can do this by regularly adding words of specific and deserved commendation to their storehouse of self-esteem. A backdrop of honest praise also facilitates the giving of occasional reproof.

Let us now examine some of the typical blocks that rob us of richer relationships with each other and keep us from further fulfilling the second great commandment.

1. Some of us have a tendency to use others, even for beneficial purposes, without their consent or in ways that are inappropriate. Remember the simple but searching self-query suggested earlier: "Whose needs am I trying to meet?" To answer honestly is to achieve some emancipating empathy. T. S. Eliot said of *false* self-esteem:

"Half of the harm that is done in this world
Is due to people who want to feel important.
They don't mean to do harm—but the harm does
    not interest them.
Or they do not see it, or they justify it
Because they are absorbed in the endless struggle
To think well of themselves."

2. Some of us in our busyness end up knowing each other as functions instead of as individuals. It is difficult

to love a function or to regard a robot. Knowing takes time. Being too busy and being too lazy mean there are some great associational adventures we will never have.

3. Some of us do not provide time or take thought for renewal or enrichment of even good relationships. Even good relationships suffer from neglect. Pressing forward through small, sweet salients (phone calls, letters, luncheons) will, more than we know, provide us with ripening relationships.

4. Some of us too often make the mistake of putting our relationships at the mercy of schedules and circumstances. Like it or not, we do experience people fatigue as well as physical fatigue. As often as not, our partners and families tend to get what is left at the end of a busy day or week. Our most important relationships deserve some prime time. Sometimes those who need our prime time the most will not in their modesty or role reluctance be the highest bidders, and we will have to go out of our way to accommodate such.

When our minds and hearts are assaulted by competing needs, it is sometimes necessary to contain our concerns, so that the individual who has the next five minutes with us is not intruded upon by carryover concerns from the individual who had the last five minutes or by our anguishing in advance over the person coming in a half hour. Little "greenbelts" of time between communicating or counseling sessions are helpful, for renewal usually requires some respite, too.

5. Some of us refuse to acknowledge growth, change, and improvement in others. Some of us let the past lock us in, rigidly refusing to reclassify other people, which can be devastating to the development of anyone. We must permit others to press forward, too.

Not only does true love refuse to rejoice when others go wrong; it also rejoices in growth and goodness regardless of the past. Better behavior deserves reinforcing responses. The past must not hold the future hostage; otherwise, what of the sons of Mosiah? Or Saul of Tarsus? Or many of us?

6. Some of us will not let another's idea have a life of its own. Rather we let the sponsorship of an idea immediately create a mind set for or against it. Sponsorship is not irrelevant, but it should not be automatically controlling. President N. Eldon Tanner does a remarkable job of letting ideas have a life of their own, including his. It is a sign of unusual wisdom and security.

7. Some of us seek to control others instead of letting them grow. Controlling is, in a sense, keeping one's brother--constraining and hedging him in. Some of us want to tie people to us even if it means limiting their possibilities instead of encouraging and helping them on their way. There is great satisfaction in helping to "launch" another person who may rise to heights we ourselves may not have achieved. Real brothers are real boosters.

8. Some of us handle poorly the challenge that occurs when others disappoint us. Just as people sometimes need love the most when they deserve it the least, so people who have disappointed us may need our love and concern most at the very moment when they have disappointed us. Disappointing behavior probably reflects some deep, unmet need in the life of a brother, a need we might help to supply. Our circles of concern need to be large and resilient enough so that--so far as others are concerned—their errors cannot take them beyond our brotherhood.

9. Some of us worry too much about differences that arise even in excellent relationships. Dealing with such differences in as ego-free a way as possible is the objective, of course. More often than we care to admit, our differences reflect expressions of ego and preferences, though we like to think of ourselves as upholding principles when differences arise.

So often the needed harmony comes from a blending--not a rejecting--of views. But even when the differences do represent real conceptual collisions, there can still be resolution with respect, which is almost always aided by genuine listening. Inspiration so often follows information; greater love so often follows added listening.

10. Some of us are not the good brothers and sisters we should be in those circumstances when a friend is being criticized. Our conduct must rise above the morality of the chicken coop in which, once a chicken is wounded, all the other chickens peck away at its bloody head. If only we could simply remember that while we need to deal frankly with mistakes (our own and those of others) when people have erred, they need us more than ever. We can offer support without approving of the error.

Since God can reveal things to a sensitive conscience that are not receivable by the keenest intellect, in such trying circumstances the heart is often more helpful than the head.

As in all things, we can look to Jesus with regard to relationships. Jesus was constant in principle, and yet He was able to particularize His relationships with others in order to help them achieve and grow in the very ways that were most important for those individuals.

There are jobs that must be done, to be sure, but being too task-oriented usually ends with our being impatient and exclusionary. Jesus not only got His great "job" done, but he kept His team virtually intact *and* prepared them for their future personal performances at the same time.

Whether or not we like to face it, it is true altogether too often that when we finally move ahead alone to do a task, because others seem unwilling to rally and in order to get the job done, others have not left us but we have left them. We ran out on them when we ran out of patience and empathy. This false sense of the lonely leader "climbing upward in the night" can be dangerous.

More often than we deserve, we like to think of ourselves as being like Uriah when his comrades deserted him in the heat of the battle.

Jesus never deserted his disciples, for even in reproof, He always spoke the truth *in love.* He also gave those about Him specific and demanding things to do, which indicated His belief that they *could* stretch their souls and *could* achieve. Ordinary people would not do extraordinary things if only ordinary challenges were put in their path.

Jesus was concerned with service, not status. If we seek clues to further progress, even though real progress is being made, there are the nearly jarring but wise and encouraging words of the Lord given to some of His disciples early in this dispensation. He told these individuals that they must strip themselves of their *jealousies* and *fears* and be more *humble*. (D&C 67:10.) For us to be freed from our fears is to reassert our command over ourselves--to be able to direct our energy, concerns, thoughts, and talents into productive paths. For us to jettison our jealousies is to stop yet another form of waste, for we cannot go where He is if we worry rather than rejoice over who else will be there. Jousting for position among peers and friends is to waste what could better be used in the battle against the enemy of evil. To be more humble includes being more teachable. There is so much to learn.

Jealousy and jousting among peers is reminiscent of a brother whose anxiety over his ascendency took him to the depths of darkness. The only things we should really fear are those things which can keep us from going where there is no fear. Adultery, yes! Death, no! Loss of righteousness, yes. Loss of status, no. Of course, one might fear the loss of a job, but hopefully not so much that he would lose his integrity while trying to keep the job. Proximate things must not maul ultimate things.

Jesus helped to prepare those about Him for the things that were to come, *without* making them so fearful and so anxious about what was impending that they were immobilized by their prospects.

Jesus prayed for those about Him--*specifically*. How often do we do this? Generalized prayers abound.

Jesus listened. When we listen only superficially to others, it is usually because we are too intent on framing what we want to say and are too concerned with "scoring" ourselves to cheer promptly and appropriately the sayings of another.

Jesus taught both explicitly and tacitly. Some leaders are reluctant to teach openly because of a false sense of modesty. We have all learned some lessons that need to be shared by explanation as well as example. It is good discipline for one to frame, express, and, if necessary, defend his generalizations.

In all ways, of course, Jesus did everything perfectly. We may feel His is an example that is far out of our reach, but His style and His principles can be applied by us even if we apply them imperfectly. Indeed, whatever the distance, we will draw nearer to Him only by following His style and principles.

How stark the contrast is between Cain's peevish reply, "Am I my brother's keeper" and the feelings of Jonathan for David, concerning which we read: "The soul of Jonathan was *knit* with the soul of David, and Jonathan loved him *as his own soul.*" (1 Samuel 18:1. Italics added.)

To be knitted with others is freeing and satisfying only if there is a correct common cause and pure love involved. Brotherhood born only of transient circumstance seldom lasts when such circumstances dissolve nor does it see beyond such circumstance.

Only when we approach the point where we see others with the same honest concern with which we see ourselves are we building relationships in which we serve and love others Jonathan-like--as our own soul. Longitudinal love--which spans circumstances and crosses cultures and generations--springs only from divinely implanted capacities that we can develop, for we are the spirit children of God the Father, who is perfect in His love.

True love of others, as well as self, will take most of us a lifetime and much more, but it is a journey that even in its early stages can be filled with great satisfactions. If we don't love our neighbor as ourselves, we may one day betray him, just as we betray ourselves when we do not live in accordance with the highest principles that we know.

God can bless us to be better brothers and better sisters if we openly and sincerely acknowledge the reality of the brotherhood of man as something more than a sweet-sounding slogan.

Perhaps our desire for credit (which often disrupts our relationships with others) arises in part from our need for a feeling of causality as much as from a need for glory. But even so, in those circumstances *we know* what we have done, and we have, if needed, the additional assurance that there is very good bookkeeping "upstairs." Why does it matter so much that others, here and now, know about what we have done? No matter how we diagnose the craving for credit, it turns out to be an unflattering explanation.

So often our compliance with the second commandment is adversely affected when our relationships involve us in power and authority roles. Some unusual guidance has been given to us in this regard.

In the Doctrine and Covenants, section 121, we read how power and influence and leadership should be maintained by the priesthood and presumably by all those who have other forms of power and authority. There is given us in this section a promise that if we do things correctly, we "shall greatly enlarge the soul without hypocrisy, and without guile. . . ." (D&C 121:42.) This suggests how the true enlargement of one's soul occurs.

These verses (41-46) also by implication warn us that we can experience an artificial enlargement of the soul when we are swollen with hypocrisy and/or guile. Hypocrisy can give us a bloated sense of our importance and of our righteousness, a distorted sense of our capacity and our goodness. Guile can fill us with an eagerness to believe the worst and with incorrect and insensitive indignation, so that instead of loving others, we become filled with animus and with envy. In such circumstances, it is easy to confuse pride with real power.

It is significant, too, that these verses emphasize Christlike conduct—persuasion, long-suffering, gentleness, meekness, love unfeigned, kindness, etc. Not only are these the qualities one needs in order to grow, but they are also the very virtues needed by us to help to produce real growth in others.

One way of seeing the importance of this grand revelation is simply to substitute the antonyms of these enumerated virtues. We should maintain power and influence by manipulation, not persuasion; by impatience, not long-suffering; by violence, not gentleness; by aggressiveness, not meekness; by pretended love and artificial affection, not love unfeigned; by hostility, not kindness; and by ignorance, not pure knowledge.

If one steps back shuddering from those antonyms, it is because the antonyms describe how worldly influence usually operates. The world is inordinately influenced by conduct and by leadership based on negative characteristics. Because such influence is so pervasive, it tends to reproduce itself in the followers of those with near-Satanic styles. One can be certain that when Satan pled for power in the premortal world and promised that he would save everybody, his technique and his "how" would have included manipulation, violence, and artificial affection! We would have lost our individuality and ended up in a cemetery of sameness.

Christlike conduct may not always be immediately contagious, but anyone who has experienced it will never forget it. Recipients of this kind of righteous influence know, experientially, that there is a better way, even if they are not able themselves to follow always in that path. Knowing that it can be done and that such conduct is possible is incredibly important. What is reachable for some is also reachable for all.

Power and influence are to be maintained with pure knowledge. Pure knowledge is knowledge that is completely valid and completely true. It is also knowledge that is very important. We see in the world some who seek to lead with a mixture of one part cleverness and one part manipulation, mixed with a tablespoon of truth.

When we see secular leaders possessed of even some good traits, we are inclined to hail them if not canonize them. This ought to tell us something about the paucity and the rarity of these combinations, and about how deep is mankind's need for such leaders. The Lord also urges us to "let thy bowels also be full of charity towards all men, and to the household of faith." One wonders why the words "and to the household of faith" were added. Yet is it not sometimes true that certain individuals love mankind generally, but not their neighbor? Is it not sometimes true that those who are proximate to us (as close as our families) receive less of our love than some of those who are more distant from us? Our circle of love and concern must move outward from those closest to us "towards all men"--not the other way around. We ought to be as nice to Church members as we are to others.

It is significant, too, in that same master revelation that we are to "let virtue garnish [our] thoughts unceasingly," for "then shall [our] confidence wax strong in the presence of God." We can't have confidence in the Lord's presence without the very virtues that would make us feel at home in that condition, including clean minds. Then and only then can we have the Holy Ghost as our "constant companion," rather than as an important, but irregular, intercessor. Improper passions leave little room for anything else, but virtue and purity make place for charity.

The "everlasting dominion" that will come to such individuals is such that "without compulsory means it shall flow unto them forever and ever." Nothing needs to be forced, for those who understand true liberty. Allegiance, love, and obedience will also flow from others to such leaders without compulsion--because the leaders' lives are based on everlasting and eternal values. People will be drawn to them just as the followers of King

Mosiah "did esteem him, yea, exceedingly, beyond measure." (Mosiah 29:40.)

In the Church we get experience both as leaders and as followers, as givers and as takers. Therefore, one of the other important skills we each need to develop is the skill of receiving. George MacDonald reminded us that "we must accept righteous sacrifices as well as make them." We must be willing to receive from others, just as we count on their receiving what we have to offer. Some parents, for instance, are so busy as givers to their children that no opportunity is provided for the parents to receive from their children. We learn about giving only by giving, and so it is also with receiving.

We need the Church for its ordinances; we need the Church for its priesthood and authority; we need the Church also because it is organized love. The Church helps us to achieve heights that we simply could not reach if we were left alone to our random impulses to do good. We need the contagion of each other's commitment. And we need each other's love!

The sense we may have at times of being devoured by duty, especially when others are slack in doing their duty, is at least partially avoidable. But as with so many real solutions, we will not hear of them, thinking them too simple. We are so unwilling to condescend to do the obvious. We could, if we chose more often, delegate, thus developing others, including our children, more and, finally, thereby reducing unnecessary burdens on ourselves.

Why do we resist the obvious, to delegate and to develop, so frequently? For many reasons. Among them:

1. We would really rather do it ourselves.

2. We are not really willing to use our time and talents in order to train others so they can help.

3. We dislike asking others to help, forgetting that receiving help is as much a part of the gospel as giving help.

4. We like to feel a bit harried because it gives us a false sense of being noble.

5. We say we are concerned about "quality control" if the task is delegated, and sometimes there is good reason for the concern; other times, however, we actually worry not about tasks being done poorly, but too well.

With regard to developing empathy, there are some techniques that can help. Suppose the aging person driving the car in front of us and responding too slowly to changing traffic signals could be regarded not as an obstruction in our path, but as our own aging mother or father? Would we honk so quickly then? Would we make allowances for the reduced alacrity of the aging?

Suppose the irritating teenager down the street who seems so insubordinate on occasion were to be regarded as our own son or daughter? Would this not call for a different reaction?

Suppose the old person who unintentionally speaks more loudly in a meeting than he needs to without realizing how disruptive that is were to be regarded as yourself a few years hence? Would there not be more understanding and patience with such a brother?

Jesus suggested this enlarged empathy when he hung on the cross and said to his disciples, "Behold thy mother!" (John 19:27.) Of course that was a pleading for his disciples to care for his mother, Mary, but it was also a reminder to us all about how we should regard mothers around us.

Another suggestion: From time to time, we can inventory those about us who seldom receive praise or expressions of appreciation and make it a point to give them deserved, specific praise. We can be especially aware of those in menial tasks or tasks that tend to be regarded as something most anyone could do. One wonders in this respect if Judas, who had such low self-esteem anyway, didn't find preoccupation with the purse and with things financial in the little kingdom somewhat lustreless. Of course, he may have preferred those duties too much, but perhaps he felt a little like the neglected ward clerk. None of this is said to justify Judas's dastardly deed, but it reminds us there are both crises of esteem and crises of faith going on around us. Usually a crisis of faith involves a crisis of self-esteem. And we can do much more, and more regularly, to build the self-esteem of others than we do.

When Jesus was in the household of Martha, an episode occurred with which we are all familiar. Martha "was cumbered about much serving." The word *cumbered* means harassed. All of us have felt this feeling at times and perhaps can feel a certain sympathy with Martha in this respect. In such circumstances, Jesus' perfect response suggests that we often need a friend, a brother, a sister, who can give us needed perspective as Jesus gave perspective to Martha. Jesus deliberately credited Martha with being "careful," acknowledging the sincerity of her effort to serve. He noted, further, that she was "troubled about many things." But then He called attention to the priority in that circumstance in which Martha's sister Mary "hath chosen that good part, which shall not be taken away from her." (Luke 10:40-42.) This situation involved a nonrecurring event in which the Lord of the earth was in their village and in their household. For Mary to have sat at Jesus' feet to hear His words didn't reflect her laziness, but her precious perspective about a moment that would not come again.

That scripture is an important scripture for all of us who at times get too task oriented and who, in the midst of our frustrations and harassments, pass it along, and sometimes with gusto, to others who seemingly are less involved than we are, who seem not to be doing their share as they should.

Some mothers in today's world feel "cumbered" by home duties and are thus attracted by other more "romantic" challenges. Such women could make the same error of perspective and priorities that Martha made. The woman, for instance, who deserts the cradle in order to help defend civilization against the barbarians may well later meet, among the barbarians, her own neglected child.

The modern Marthas may include those who are careful and troubled by many things, some deservedly. But they needlessly leave kitchen and cradle not for instruction by the selfless Savior of mankind, but for self-serving enterprises that will be distance-producing as far as their primary relationships are concerned.

There are some useful ways to test the value of relationships. This can best be done by applying the principles taught by Jesus and His prophets.

The opposite of the sweet relationship of Ruth and Naomi or David and Jonathan is the relationship of Laman and Lemuel. The pathos of the poor Lemuels of the world may be the greatest of all. Lemuel appeared not to have a thought or mind of his own, for, we read, "he hearkened unto the words of Laman." (1 Nephi 3:28.) Serious sinners who regard themselves as free are the most obvious satellites in our human solar system. If one is going to be a satellite, he had better pick his Saturns carefully. Indeed, followership in the kingdom leaves no place for static, satellite relationships, for individual growth based on eternal principles is the criterion. To mix metaphors, Pied Piper situations are not only hard on the followers but are bad for the Pied Pipers too.

Peter grew as his devotion to Jesus grew. President Brigham Young's last words before death were "Joseph, Joseph, Joseph!" The growth of the glazier from Vermont into a colonizer-prophet bespeaks not a mindless sublimation to the Prophet Joseph, but a fertile fellowship. In discipleship, intentions are not enough, including the intent to communicate. President Brigham Young candidly said, "I feel it sometimes very difficult indeed to word my thoughts as they exist in my own mind, which, I presume, is the grand cause of many apparent differences in sentiment which may exist among the Saints." (*Journal of Discourses* 2:123.) President Young cared about both his people and his communications with them.

We do know more than we can tell. We so often have

ideas we cannot frame fully in words. Knowing this at least sensitizes us to the need to allow others the same latitude, for they too may find it difficult to frame their thoughts and ideas with sufficient precision that they will always be understood. Thus as we communicate we *must* speak the truth in love, for the love and good intent will come across even if our concept or idea is poorly framed.

It is largeness of soul that permits us to pay attention to small things, because in life as in marriage, the little things are the big things. Since little things are so vital, it is no wonder that it is usually the little things that get to us, causing us to break stride in the press forward. The ward choir director may wish the monotone in the choir would reduce his volume, but the monotone is placing his best voice on the altar of Church service! Likewise, we can and should have more reverence in our chapels and foyers, but isn't it good that the increase in the decibel level when we are together occurs because of good feelings rather than bad ones?

Another irritant to brotherhood is the way in which our little faults are brought to our attention when it is least convenient and also by someone who has so many of his own! Yet we should be glad, if only later, for the warnings from fellow travelers, regardless of whether or not these warnings are given in good grammar. These warnings are like having a friend tell us just in time that we are mistakenly carrying matches as we are about to enter an explosives factory.

Even coping with the conscientiousness of others is a test. There are those who, whatever their calling in the Church, come to feel that their calling is *the* major task in the Church. Somehow as they magnify their calling, other callings, in their view, seem to shrink in significance. Great care must be taken not to put down such individuals, for surely enthusiasm is better than passivity, but since so many callings converge at the point of member duties, great care must also be taken to exercise some restraint.

Work multiplied is sometimes like words multiplied. It is one thing for me to magnify my own effectiveness in my calling; it is quite another for me to misconstrue magnification to mean that others must do much more because I must meet my ego needs in my new calling.

Such situations involve very delicate balances within the framework of the second commandment, but there are some helping graces: the doer must balance the demands made of others with the demands made of himself; the called person must endeavor to influence higher performance in others by his example rather than by his ego; we must be as careful in budgeting the time asked of Church members as we are in budgeting the expenditure of their other resources; and finally, let us acknowledge that discipleship does involve difficult decisions even in the deployment of our own time, talent, and means—and hence even more challenges when the deployment involves others as well as ourselves.

Lest our advocacy for a particular program or emphasis become too absolute, we should remember, indeed we have an obligation not to forget, our similar feelings when in a previous calling, and we should realize that ere long we will be caught up (and properly so) in yet another calling. The very governance of the Church and rotation in assignments provides some good checks and balances, but meanwhile, for us, draining off ego considerations and replacing these with empathy creates a good context for our conscientiousness.

Our spirit of self-sufficiency is never stronger than when things seem to be going well and we seem not to need God so much. One does not usually appreciate being jostled out of such moments, and he may glare at the jostler. Contrariwise, when we feel insecure and unready, it may be a friend (or even a stranger) who knocks off our training wheels and sends us gasping but succeeding—on our way!

Building brotherhood and struggling to keep the second commandment can also help us avoid unproductive worry. Some of us spend time and talent, as well as energy, worrying over what never befalls us. A loving family and friends can give us perspective if we will heed them. Unjustified anxiety is another of the devil's diversions; it can be coped with by having friends who can speak the truth to us in love or who can show us the serenity midst stress that we have yet to achieve.

Without the associational advantages of the Church we would not get much experience, either, in seeing how vital it is that we really come to believe, under certain conditions, that God can forgive us. If we do not so believe, it is useless to speak of forgiving each other. Just as without God there cannot be any real wrongs or rights (just the chameleon codes of mortal lawmakers), so only when we are forgiven by Him can we appreciate how sweet and needed that same feeling is for others.

The commingling of our prayers also teaches us about brotherhood. We become more conscious, for instance, of the provincialism of our prayers. It is our provincialism that causes us to pray for things not in our best interest--like the farmer eager for just a little more rain to swell his crops who prays for more rain without realizing that the earth-fill dam up the canyon from his farm will collapse with just a little more rain.

Naturally, in developing our brotherhood we are asked to do difficult things. These tasks would simply be too hard to do if we did not know and trust a loving Father. And some of the hardest lessons are given to those farthest along the trail. Sweet and mighty Moses was, we recall, not permitted to go over into the promised land--he was permitted only a peek from atop Pisgah, "for thou shalt not go over this Jordan." (Deuteronomy 3:27.) Was not that enough to demand of that precious disciple of the desert? No, for there was more: Moses was then asked to aid and help his successor, Joshua, who *would* lead Israel over into the promised land: "But charge Joshua, and encourage him, and strengthen him: for he shall go over before this people, and he shall cause them to inherit the land which thou shalt see." (Deuteronomy 3:28.)

Moses did as he was asked out of *obedience* but also out of rich *brotherhood.*

How often in Church life we need both in order to do what must be done! How often releases and missionary transfers seem to come just barely before a new milestone is to be passed! How often successors reap where others have planted, but resentments are either nonexistent or minimal because of prevailing brotherhood and confidence in authority!

Sometimes keeping the second great commandment means giving others a second chance when their critics are not so generous. President Heber J. Grant was made president of the Tooele Stake at age twenty-four. Later that same day when one of the Brethren asked the young stake president if he had an absolute testimony, the reply was not an absolute testimony. The conscientious and surprised General Authority then remarked in the presence of President John Taylor that young President Grant should be released. A wise President Taylor chuckled and said, ". . . he knows it just as well as you do. The only thing that he does not know is that he does know it. It will be but a short time until he does know it," and noted that all concerned should simply give Heber some time to realize it. (*Improvement Era,* July 1939, p. 393.) In a sense, a future president of the Church hung in the balance, but he had a wise brother willing to stand by him and to trust in his possibilities, for President Grant himself described his shaky start as a stake president.

The quality of our love and concern for our fellowmen can often be measured in seemingly little ways. For instance, if we are so task-oriented that we murmur at a busy intersection because a siren-wailing ambulance comes through that intersection on "our" green light, then we have forgotten the needs of another, putting our convenience ahead of his necessity.

Of muttering and murmuring generally, perhaps it needs to be said that if we were honest, we would admit that, in those circumstances, we say what we say in the manner that we say it *because* we want to go on record but not too loudly. Perhaps, too, we want it known that we have already gone the first mile!

We do seem to have developed a strange sense of "territory" concerning our time and our talents; we may not post "no trespassing" signs, but we like people to come through the front gate and not unannounced and uninvited over our fences.

If we are glad when others go wrong because that improves our competitive position, we need to heed what Elder Boyd K. Packer has said: "We get conditioned to the idea that only one team or one person can win. This is not true of spiritual things. There is plenty of room in the Celestial Kingdom for everyone. We are not in competition for some few spaces. The only one we are in competition with is our former self."

If we find it difficult to hold up the outstretched hand of a friend when the conversational tide washes over him, we may be a fair-weather friend, for he needs us then, not when the waspish waves have ceased running.

It can be helpful on occasions to ask ourselves, "How would I behave and what would I say, if what happens in the next few minutes were to occur in a theater-in-the-round with all involved present to hear what I am about to say and do?" Would the friend fare better? Would we be so quick to engage in conversational cloak-holding? Whether we are prepared to admit it or not, most of us are actually counting on our friends' being more generous to us in such circumstances than we are being to them!

It is not that the frailties of friends are absent or that their deficiencies are irrelevant; rather, more often than we do, it would be better for us to notice and absorb without comment, rather than both noticing *and* commenting—a little more reticence to rush to judgment, a point, by the way, that has been made several times in the scriptures on which we are to feast regularly.

A healthy regard for God, life, neighbor, and self requires the full acceptance of precious truths about God, man, and the universe. If, for instance, we deny the existence of a loving Eternal Father and the divinity of Jesus Christ, and if we cannot accept the existence of the plan of life, we have not only cut loose from the first and second great commandments, but from *all* the law and prophets that hang upon these two commandments!

Fortunately, God neither stops existing nor loving because a mere mortal rejects Him. So far as nonbelievers are concerned, we must not reject them because they reject our message.

The more one searches the truths in the gospel, the more the wonder. Just as scientists in their exploration of matter have found that with a new verity there comes a new vista (first the marvels of the molecule, then the awe of the atomic order, now the splendor of the sub-atomic world), so it is with the seamless structure of the gospel. There are no welds or cracks, nor any ultimate contradictions. We encounter imponderables, yes, but only as we come upon a new truth that past illumination did not reveal to us. The imponderables of today then become tomorrow's immense insight.

And in no dimension of the gospel are the wonder and joy greater than in the disciple's compliance with the first and second great commandments.

Chapter Seven

ON ENDURING WELL TO THE END

My son, peace be unto thy
soul; thine adversity and thine afflictions shall
be but a small moment; And then, if thou
endure it well, God shall exalt thee on high.
(Doctrine and Covenants 121:7-8.)
. . . know thou, my son, that
all these things shall give thee experience,
and shall be for thy good.
(Doctrine and Covenants 122:7.)
Beloved, think it not strange concerning
the fiery trial which is to try you, as
though some strange
thing happened unto you.
(1 Peter 4:12.)
. . . God said that He would have
a tried people,
that He would purge them as gold.
(Joseph Smith, HC 3:294.)

To think of enduring to the end as "hanging in there," doing one's duty relentlessly, is not inaccurate. Yet enduring to the end is more than outlasting and surviving, though it includes those qualities. We are called upon, as was the Prophet Joseph, to "endure it well," gracefully, not grudgingly. (D&C 121:8.) We are also told that we must "endure in faith." (D&C 101:35.) These dimensions of enduring are important to note. Likewise, we are asked to endure "valiantly." (D&C 121:29.)

The Savior said, "Look unto me, and endure to the end." (3 Nephi 15:9.) The quality of enduring could scarcely be achieved unless we did "look unto" Christ.

The poet-prophet Jacob speaks of the saints as having "endured the crosses of the world" (2 Nephi 9:18) and as having "despised the shame" of the world. Obviously, this involves more than coping with the mere passage of time. What are the "crosses of the world"? We cannot be sure, but the imagery suggests the bearing of a cross placed upon us by the world, as Jesus did; there may be persecutors and unhelpful onlookers, and the Church member is set apart (if not set upon), yet he does not flinch when accused and scoffed at by those who would make him ashamed, for he has no real reason to be ashamed.

It is best not to try to delineate too precisely between the crosses of the world and the cares of the world. The former may press us down, while the latter divert us. But the outcome is the same––the climb is stopped; instead of overcoming, we have been overcome.

We need also to have faith in and to be supportive of all callings, including our own. President Marion G. Romney movingly and humbly told the members of his home ward, at the time of his original call to the First Presidency, that he had faith in all those whom the Lord calls including the call that had just come to him. Enduring the sense of our inadequacy in the face of callings is more common than we know.

We are also asked to endure temptation. (James 1:12.) The growing coarseness of our times suggests that, like Lot in Sodom, we may be "vexed with the filthy conversation of the wicked" (2 Peter 2:7)––just one more way in which we must endure evil in our environments.

But does not God know beforehand if we can endure? Yes, perfectly. But *we* need to know, firsthand, about our capacity. So much of a life well lived consists of coming to know what God knows already. Could our joy be complete if our personal triumph were not complete? Could we have the self-esteem necessary for the heavier––much heavier––duties to devolve upon us in that better world, if we did not know personally that we had passed the test and had fought the good fight?

Meanwhile, the tests so often consist of vexing little things. The harassed helper, especially if he believes he has not been appreciated lately, is vulnerable. Since we really are to be the servants of others, some things can be done to help us to endure well the complexity and volume of problems others bring to us.

1. Focusing questions sincerely asked of others ("How can I be of specific help?" "You have obviously thought about this very much. What are your recommendations?") can avoid the "stream of consciousness" form of communication that not only wastes time, but also usually requires focusing questions later anyway.

2. Noting how important the next thirty minutes will be is also a reminder to others about the limits of the appointment, when such limits need to be set.

3. Blocking out time for family and personal renewal is vital, and, barring emergencies, plans can be subtly communicated by a quorum president to his counselors, who can do some steering of the "traffic." Those needing help are usually understanding of this need to keep faith with one's family.

4. Making certain that the pyramid process (helping others at the level closest to them before going to the next level) is used lovingly and consistently can do much to protect, for instance, the busy bishop or stake Relief Society President. It was Jethro who noted a second and more hidden danger in the failure to delegate—not only would the leader "wear away," but the people would "wear away" too. Counseling delayed may be counseling denied so far as the critical moment is concerned.

5. Making certain that in terms of voice tone, posture, and facial feedback we give others the best we have when they are with us provides them with a quality quarter of an hour instead of a half-hearted hour.

The disciple can be assured that when the basic virtues are in the process of active development, the techniques can also be developed. Since technique is tied to personal style and to circumstances, this volume has spoken only sparingly of technique. Suffice it to say, however, that our techniques should always be tested against principle. Techniques must not become little tricks we play on ourselves or others. Techniques such as those involved in enduring well must be grounded in the gospel. Ends require means, but means that are consistent with the ends being served.

Endurance is even more than elasticized courage, for it underwrites all the other virtues across the expanse of life. Without endurance, the other virtues would be episodic; faith would be fitful, and virtue transitory.

We will not have in all specific situations the answers to questions such as "Why me?" "Why this?," but knowing the grand "why" of life will help us to endure the gritty little "whys" of this month or this year.

With gospel perspective, we can know that when we endure *to the very end*, we are actually enduring *to the very beginning*. Thus, rather than viewing this virtue as delivering us expiring in exhaustion to a finish line, we are brought intact and victorious to a starting line!

In the words of the Prophet Joseph Smith, we "hope to be able to endure all things." (Article of Faith 13.) While we are not out looking for things to endure, some tests seem more likely to come our way in addition to those already mentioned.

We will live in a time of great lust not unlike another when it was said to an evil people, "How shall I pardon thee for this? thy children have forsaken me, and sworn by them that are no gods: when I had fed them to the full, they then committed adultery, and assembled themselves by troops in the harlots' houses. They were as fed horses in the morning: every one neighed after his neighbour's wife." (Jeremiah 5:7-8.)

The very crassness of worldly ways, once the hardening has reached a certain point, is such that shame is no longer possible. Such a time had apparently been reached in the days of Jeremiah when, speaking of the evils among the people, he asked, "Were they ashamed when they had committed abomination? nay, they were not at all ashamed, neither could they blush: therefore they shall fall among them that fall: . . . Thus saith the Lord, Stand ye in the ways, and see, and ask for the old paths, where is the good way, and walk therein, and ye shall find rest for your souls. . . ." (Jeremiah 6:15-16.) The phrasing of Jeremiah is significant in our time. He speaks of the people who had lost their capacity to walk in old paths and to blush. Sound familiar? Indeed this description sounds like a people who had not only departed from the ways of the Lord, but who also "loved to have it so."

If in these times there seem to be more warnings than in other ages, it is because this is not a time when there can be many words. When someone is about to step into the path of an oncoming truck, the individual giving the warning does not take time to explain the make, model, and color of the truck that is coming or indeed to mention the velocity. He simply shouts! There is often no time to do more regarding some of the trends in our society.

This is an age, too, when it may again be necessary for leaders to do what leaders did once before in Book of Mormon times, to bear down in "pure testimony" so people will know clearly what their choices are. In a time around eighty-four years before Christ, there were among the people of the Church "envyings, and strife, and malice, and persecutions, and pride, even to exceed the pride of those who did not belong to the church of God." (Alma 4:9.)

The Church did not progress. Indeed the wickedness in some of the members of the Church was "a great stumbling-block to those who did not belong to the church." (Alma 4:10.) In such a setting Alma retained the office of high priest in the Church and gave up "the judgment-seat unto Nephihah." (Alma 4:18.) Alma did this because he saw clearly what was necessary. He freed himself in terms of his time so that he might "preach the word of God unto them, to stir them up in remembrance of their duty, and that he *might pull down, by the word of God,* all the pride and craftiness and all the contentions which were among his people, seeing no way that he might reclaim them save it were in *bearing down in pure* testimony against them." (Alma 4:19. Italics added.)

That society was sufficiently far gone that it was too late to turn it around by debates in a Parliament and by this or that judicial decision. The people had to be told, and told plainly, of the peril they faced.

Of course, this does not mean that warnings cannot be given in love or that the testimonies cannot be born in genuine love and affection. Even the warnings that must be delivered abruptly can be given, indeed should be given, with the truth being spoken, as Paul counseled us, in love. People can often respond at first to our love and to our concern more than to the content of our message. The quality of our lives can make it so much easier for people to believe on our words. When they have heard the gospel from us, they may say as a queenly woman said, "I have had no witness save thy word . . . nevertheless I believe." (Alma 19:9.)

Given the kind of high adventure that we know is coming to us such as is contained in the prophecy of Heber C. Kimball, we must be prepared to speak plainly. President Kimball said that prior to the rebuilding of the Church in Missouri, "The Saints will be put to tests that will try the integrity of the best of them. The pressure will become so great that the more righteous among them *will cry unto the Lord day and night until deliverance comes."* (*Deseret News,* Church Section, May 23, 1931, p. 3. Italics added.)

Difficulties of this degree will be experienced before traumatic deliverance comes. In such circumstances, what we say must be said plainly though lovingly. There is no time for sophistry or games or cleverness. Somehow in such circumstances, the proper balance will be struck by the prophets who will see that the gospel is carried to all nations "for a witness" in which we focus on preaching "Christ and him crucified," so that other less important things do not get in the way of that grand message. At the same time there will apparently be, according to President Brigham Young, a very special effort made. President Young said, "I expect to see the day when the Elders of Israel will protect and sustain civil and religious liberty and every constitutional right bequeathed to us by our fathers, and spread those rights abroad in connection with the Gospel for the salvation of all nations." (*Journal of Discourses* 11:262-63.) But such an added emphasis would come only by prophetic direction.

These prophetic comments were made in an address in the Bowery in Salt Lake City August 12, 1866. President Young had just listened to an address by Elder George A. Smith, who had apparently recapitulated something of the history and suffering of the Church and its people and their coming to the Salt Lake Valley. President Young was able to be forgiving and ecumenical in the face of those memories and observed: "I am thankful that the rehearsal of those occurrences has ceased to irritate me as it did formerly." (*JD* 11:257.) He had risen above the harsh history that had brought the Saints to that valley and the afflictions that had accompanied their pioneer passage.

We should not be dismayed if our words are reacted to as the words of earlier leaders were reacted to in Old Testament times. We read this searing indictment with regard to the insensitivity of earlier inhabitants: "But they mocked the messengers of God, and despised his words, and misused his prophets, . . . *till there was no remedy.*" (2 Chronicles 36:16. Italics added.)

But enduring, as already indicated, consists of much more than just coping with the passage of time or putting up with things we cannot change, though these are a part of enduring. We must, for instance, endure in doing good without becoming weary in well-doing--a special challenge in declining times when we may be tempted to think the good done is of no consequence.

Another special challenge we face from time to time is having good motives and good intentions--and even good actions misfire. Abish, the "Lamanitish woman"

(Alma 19:16-17), was not the first nor the last Church member to think an opportunity to be present and, therefore, to act on the impulse to do good. Confusion and contention followed her deed, as did tears from conscientious Abish. Vindication was nearly immediate in her case, but it is much slower coming at other times.

If our motives and actions are good, we should be able to endure some misunderstanding, but the pain and frustration of it will be real because we really care. Time and truth can cause lower courts of opinion to reverse themselves, hopefully soon. But if not, we will come to that final gate where Jesus Christ is the gatekeeper and "he employeth no servant there." The gospel guarantees ultimate, not proximate, justice.

A tender story told by President Marion G. Romney illustrates another aspect of enduring:

"In 1912 Father's family, with the other war refugees from the Mormon colonies in northern Chihuahua, fled into the United States. Two years later he and his brother Gaskell, with their families—Father with eight children, his brother with six—settled in Oakley, Idaho.

"Father was employed as a teacher in the Cassia Stake Academy at a salary of $80 a month. The two brothers pooled their earnings and divided their income equally.

"During the winter of 1913-14, my uncle, a carpenter, could find no employment and therefore had no income. Father's salary of $80 a month had to be divided between the families. If tithing was to be paid, each family would have $36 a month. If it was not paid, each family would have $40.

"A family council was held to decide whether to pay tithing. The decision was to pay. For me, then 16 years of age, this was a crucial decision; I thought it was unrealistic. How could our family, ten people, live on $36 a month—$3.60 each? We had to pay rent and buy fuel. Having left a warm climate and come to a cold one, we were in desperate need of clothing. I was sensitive and embarrassed by the appearance of the cast-off clothing we wore. Notwithstanding my feelings, tithing—the debt owed to the Lord—was paid and we survived the winter. Father's integrity paid off. He never compromised in dealing with me or the Lord."

Pooled tithing is like pooled talents. We can do so much more than we could ever accomplish alone, for what is being pooled is not just money, but dedication!

What our involvement in missionary work often lacks is a fixed time for accountability like tithing settlement; we are always "refinancing" our resolves, putting off the practical payments. Thank goodness for the toll-booths along the straight and narrow path that call us to account on some things!

We must also endure—by producing examples, explanations, and exhortations in order to help—the confusions of those who simply don't understand at first why the Church and the gospel mean everything to us. Such individuals often seem to be looking for something else to explain us and our devotion to the Church other than the truth.

Errors need not be great before distance and time make a very great difference in the outcome! The Old Testament scriptures concerning Jesus' advent were quite clear and each prophecy was fulfilled. But almost all missed out. How? Because they mistook the nature of the second coming for the first? Yes. Because the busy-ness of the workaday world dulled their interests and perceptions? Yes. Because they were also looking beyond the mark? Yes, indeed. But also, because having not really searched the scriptures and having not been schooled in the scriptures, they genuinely did not expect what emerged. There was the obscurity of a Nazarene prophet; the scalding criticism of Him by the establishment; no interest by Him in triumph over Rome; the leadership of fishermen instead of the Sanhedrin. How unattractive to the *cognoscente* of that time!

Those same reactions are in evidence today with regard to the Lord and his church. Some let the obscurity of The Church of Jesus Christ of Latter-day

117

Saints block their examination of its validity. Others find the bold claims of Christ's church today too much for them, just as some then could not accept Jesus' claim about who He was. Still others are put off by a smoke-screen of allegations and charges about the Church, preferring to believe the worst rather than to know the truth. Christians who would not think of judging Jesus by Judas will listen to today's Judases and defecting disciples, who seem, by the way, to do much better than Judas's thirty pieces of silver.

Indeed, our very eagerness to serve the kingdom must be carefully projected. We must not let our tongues testify beyond what we know, lest what we do know is then called into question. Paul warned Timothy that some church members had swerved aside into "vain jangling" because, apparently, they desired "to be teachers of the law; understanding neither what they say, nor whereof they affirm." (1 Timothy 1:6-7.) Likewise we must be careful not to let our desire to help buckle under the temptation to have ready answers for everything. We must learn to endure sensitively when certain answers are not available. We must also spring back from our own mistakes.

Next to avoiding mistakes, most to be admired is the quick and honest recovery from them. For instance, a miscommunication followed by "I did not say that very well, did I? May I try again?"

It is not improbable, now and then, that while we are in the very act of spreading the work of truth, trying to build up the kingdom, some unpleasant truth with personal implications may be flung at us to throw us off balance. Coping with the need to respond even when embarrassed is also a dimension of enduring. A saving or helping truth may be a bitter pill, but it is never toxic!

A wide-eyed infantryman in basic training during World War II, I saw a lieutenant, much admired by his platoon, attempt to leap upon a tank to speak to the troops. He fell and scraped his legs badly, but with no more than a wince, he quickly jumped again, this time successfully, to speak to the troops while in great pain. None of us heard what he said, but we saw what he did. Coping with our own shortfalls, even when these are painfully public, is the best sermon on our own staying-power.

We must endure the barbs of those in this age when democratic emphases are the seeming test of everything, for some will remind us that we are members of an authoritarian church. Indeed we are, and while much could be said on this subject, the author often notes to those who are critical of an authoritarian church—better to have a theocracy with a little democracy than a democracy with only a little theology. Further, can one seriously propose a church of Jesus Christ in which the King has only one vote—and each subject the same?

One great aid that is essential to enduring is to be able to have access to the promptings of the Spirit.

Sometimes we try to make access to the promptings of the Spirit an almost mechanical thing. There are so many things involved: our readiness, the need for the prompting, studying it out in our minds, taking no thought save it were to ask, lessons to be learned, etc.

The true disciple has an inborn questing to know, personally, all that God is willing to teach us. Nephi could have accepted gladly the vision of his father, Lehi. But Nephi "desired to know the things that [his] father had seen." (1 Nephi 11:1.) Abraham sought, even though he had a father who had turned from the faith, "for greater happiness and peace" and "for mine appointment unto the Priesthood." (Abraham 1:2, 4.) Abraham described himself as desiring "great knowledge, and to be a greater follower of righteousness" (Abraham 1:2), questing for the word of Christ. Divine discontent in the form of promptings can move us to feast because we know that by feasting we can increase our knowledge, effectiveness, and joy.

Now, clearly, the word of Christ, as given in the past through the holy scriptures and as given to us now through the Holy Ghost, can provide us with the guidance necessary to help us to know "all things what [we] should do." (2 Nephi 32:3.) Such can happen when the Holy Ghost is our constant companion, not a periodic partner.

There is a twin danger in our glossing over certain promises as profound as this one, however. First, we may be unduly harsh on ourselves when revelations for our personal lives do not gush forth as if from a fire hydrant. Second, we may think of the process as if it were like switching our decision-making apparatus on "automatic pilot," leaving us with a ho-hum role.

We must make allowance for the real possibility that we are lacking in faith and/or worthiness. But we must also make allowance for the equally real possibility that some considerations of growth are involved at times, too. Oliver Cowdery was told that he had oversimplified his role in the process: "You took no thought save it was to ask." (D&C 9:7.)

Next, the effort to study propositions out in our mind, carefully and prayerfully, can be followed by a stupor or a burning, but these are not the only ways in which God can tell what we should do. There is a spectrum of styles used by the Lord to inspire and guide us. If we seek to make the process too mechanical, we may deprive ourselves of guidance from God that comes in other ways, equally valid. Matthias, Judas's replacement, was chosen by lot, but no doubt under the direction of the Spirit. Dreams, visions, Urim and Thummim, voices, and some forms of revelation are quite dramatic. Yet, as the Prophet Joseph Smith said, inspiration can come in the form of "sudden strokes of ideas." President Marion G. Romney has noted how whole sentences have come into his mind. The author has said God does not send thunder when a still small voice is enough.

Inspiration can come in the form of our being directed to already revealed wisdom that is apropos and adequate for our need. The disciple needs to become at home in the Lord's library. A bit of wisdom or a phrase uttered by a friend in a timely way can remain in our mind and prove catalytic in meeting the challenge. There are probably some situations in which we are struggling over something that is a matter of preference rather than principle, or situations in which more than one alternative is acceptable and, as the Lord said on one occasion, "it mattereth not unto me." (D&C 60:5.)

Divine guidance is so crucial, however, that we need to go out of our way to put ourselves in a situation in which such special help can be given. President David O. McKay spoke of how the morning hours, before we are cluttered with the cares of day, are especially conducive to inspiration. Others have felt that solitude and reading the scriptures can create an atmosphere conducive to the Spirit and can be developed. After all, to read the words of Christ already before us is a good thing to do before asking for more. Sometimes steady importuning is a necessity.

As desirable as the frequency of revelation and inspiration is, that it happens at all is the crucial thing. In any event, we may know that a loving Father will give to us as we are ready, and even then in a way that is consistent with our need to grow and the needs of others who may be involved in the considerations at hand.

General Authorities, for instance, are not able to go to a community and live for weeks among the people before selecting a new stake president. Those circumstances, therefore, may lend themselves to more dramatic examples of direct inspiration than, say, circumstances when a mother is struggling to communicate with a daughter. The latter situation is as vital as the former and inspiration can be and is given in rich ways, but there may be growth considerations involved in the latter situation that may not obtain in the former.

Other times it is good for us to ponder more than we do. Mary, the mother of Jesus, heard and saw almost more than she could absorb for the moment, so she kept certain things in her heart and pondered them. The main thing for the disciple to do is to increase his personal righteousness, to inquire, and to be ready to re-

121

ceive. That is far more important than focusing on technique and mechanics or seeking to follow a single delivery system.

It should not surprise us that one of the highest exercises of discipleship, learning to draw upon the Spirit for help, should require some schooling—sometimes deep and extensive schooling. We may need to learn, for instance, that reflection and pause are even more necessary than we had supposed in order to wipe clean the busy chalkboard of our lives; fresh impressions need a place to be recorded. The visit to a sick friend we are prompted to make but do not make because we have our own problems, may provide a clue: often we need first to seek inspiration in order to help others *before* we ask for it to help ourselves. With regard to inspiration, as with other things in the kingdom, we must be faithful stewards over small things first.

If we desire to have the promptings of the Spirit become almost habitual in our lives, then we must develop the habits that lend themselves to the flow of such inspiration.

We should learn, too, that the prompting that goes unresponded to may not be repeated. Writing down what we have been prompted with is vital. A special thought can also be lost later in the day in the rough and tumble of life. God should not, and may not, choose to repeat the prompting if we assign what was given such a low priority as to put it aside.

Finally, regarding promptings and impressions, this is special territory one enters for which detailed maps are not available. The guides who know the country well speak of such things only in hushed tones, if at all. Suffice it to say that if we truly hunger and thirst after such things, we will be led to living water!

President John Taylor said, as if in commentary on the blending of enduring and prompting: "Pray for the revelations of God, that the spirit and power of God may rest upon us, that we may comprehend correct principles and understand the laws of life, to guide and guard and protect the ship's Zion from among the rocks and shoals and troubles that will sooner or later overcome this nation and other nations, and prepare ourselves for the events that are to come."

Indeed the pressures will be so great that the Lord will be asked to shorten the days of tribulation. "For then shall be great tribulation, such as was not since the beginning of the world to this time, no, nor ever shall be. And except those days should be shortened, there should no flesh be saved: but for the elect's sake those days shall be shortened." (Matthew 24:21-22.)

And finally, it is more than noteworthy that Nephi tells of how the Son's voice came to him to attest to the mighty responsibilities that come with the baptisms of water and fire. Then Nephi heard the voice of the Father certify to the truth of what the Son had said, saying further: "He that endureth to the end, the same shall be saved." (2 Nephi 31:15.) The Father chose to emphasize, among the many things He might have said, *enduring to the end.*

A SUMMING UP

. . . little people like you and
me, if our prayers are sometimes granted,
beyond all hope and probability, had better
not draw hasty conclusions to our own
advantage. If we were stronger, we might be
less tenderly treated. If we were braver, we
might be sent, with far less help, to defend far
more desperate posts in the great battle.
(C. S. Lewis, *The World's Last Night*
[New York: Harvest Books, 1969],
pp. 10-11.)
It is not the critic who
counts, not the man who points out how the
strong man stumbled or where the doer of
deeds could have done them better. The
credit belongs to the man who is actually in
the arena; whose face is marred by dust and
sweat and blood; who strives valiantly;
who errs and comes short again
and again; who knows the great enthusiasms,
the great devotions and spends himself
in a worthy cause; who, at the best,
knows the triumph of high achievement;
and who, at the worst, if he fails,
at least fails while daring greatly, so
that his place shall never be with those cold
and timid souls who know neither victory nor
defeat. (Theodore Roosevelt.)

Disciples, like diamonds, are developed in a process of time and heavy pressures, and both the disciple and the diamond reflect and magnify the light that comes through them.

Just as the straight and narrow path never slopes even slightly downhill, so discipleship is ascending and even agonizing. Jesus' last hours and moments were the most cruel. His prophet, Joseph Smith, underwent last hours and moments that were not filled with serene surroundings. Carthage was, for a time, a corner of hell, filled with filthy conversation that vexed his soul. Some disciples do not end their soldierly and gallant journey in a vigorous salute in a dress parade, but in halting senility or with a stroke that stretches out their days. What is God doing? What lessons are underway? We can only surmise and trust. If growth is tied to challenge—and it is—we must expect righteousness to meet resistance.

Since time is so precious a commodity, we must not be dismayed when the time permitted to savor success seems so small on occasion. High moments are soon followed by fresh challenges. It could scarcely be otherwise, for none of us would for long want to be banqueting over our blessings while others stood without, waiting for the touch of our lives and talents.

If seeing suffering that we wish we could stop, especially as it involves family and friends, is often one of the experiences of life, and it is, will not this extra agony help us in a tiny way to have a fraction of the feeling Father has known as He has experienced the suffering of His children?

Having been given the gospel frame of reference, we see life differently, others differently, and our duties differently. For instance, as we contemplate our specific responsibilities, it is significant to note that in Joseph Smith's incomplete but inspired translation of the Bible, he added these words to the renderings of Matthew 6:33: *"Wherefore, seek not the things of this world* but seek ye first *to build up* the kingdom of God, and *to establish* his righteousness, and all these things shall be added unto you." (Inspired Version, Matthew 6:38. Added words shown in italics.)

At a time when we are very much in the world, these additional words of the prophets are most sobering. We are not only to seek first the kingdom of God, but we are to "seek not the things of this world." Finally, we are "to build up" the kingdom of God. This lays heavy and specific responsibilities on us and gives us a frame of reference for life that others may find puzzling at times but that is completely consistent with the conceptual core of the gospel of Jesus Christ.

We know from modern revelation (D&C 101:39-40) that when disciples accept the gospel and make their covenants with Heavenly Father, such individuals are counted "as the salt of the earth and the savor of men." So much depends upon the small, but special, group of human beings to whom God has entrusted the spreading of the word of the building up of the kingdom of God.

Lest we feel at times a sense of dismay about challenges that face us, let us also remember that surely God, who has fixed the bounds of habitations of men, has taken care to place His restored kingdom in a situation where it would not be overrun. Surely God, who does not fail to see the death of a single sparrow, is not unmindful of the challenges of environmental evil that come to His and all people. We should content ourselves to know that all of this has been anticipated, including our ability to cope with it if we will.

Of course, there are specific things to be done, chores that require attention. It was that practical powerful man, Brigham Young, who said of one sort of challenge, "Let every individual in this city feel the same interest for the public good as he does for his own, and you will at once see this community still more prosperous and still more rapidly increasing in wealth, influence, and power, but where each one seeks to benefit himself or herself alone, and does not cherish a feeling for prosperity and benefit of the whole, that people will be disorderly, unhappy, and poverty stricken, and distress, animosity, and strife will reign." To cite but one test, it is how we cope with the challenge of urbanization, not urbanization itself, that will determine the outcome.

It is important in our relationships with our fellowmen that we approach them as neighbors and as brothers and sisters rather than coming at them flinging theological thunderbolts.

It is important, too, that we press forward in our families. Mormon marriages ought not to be marriages in which men are the theologians and women are the Christians; we must press forward together, for men cannot finally go anywhere that matters without women.

Quite clearly, we are leaving a rather calm summer sea that has been our lot lately, and we are sailing into stormy waters. We need to acknowledge the Captain on the bridge and to see to it that the portholes are closed and that everyone is at his post. There will be others who will want to come on board. These people, many of the fine people of the earth, are presently searching for light and warmth against the gathering darkness and the astral chill that blows in from the sea of skepticism.

With regard to the signs that are preceding the second coming of Jesus, most will miss them and a few will overreact. Have you ever had the experience of looking at your watch without really noting what time it was? The world in its intense preoccupation will see some of the signs preceding the second coming without really noticing them. Because our view of brotherhood is that men are not merely biological brothers--because we know that we are more than stranded passengers on an earthship that is about to blink, quiver, and die--we can accept each other in a more full and complete way. We look for the day when as children of our Father in heaven, the designations Appalachian, Asian, or American will no longer be significant, nor will using words like Dutch or Nigerian. When that day comes, salutations from our Heavenly Father to us will be "son," "daughter," and among ourselves, "brothers," "sisters."

Meanwhile, we must call attention to the true standards of righteousness––God's standards, not the world's standards––and we must lovingly jar, if necessary, those who need to be shaken into this reality. Strong doctrines must be enunciated, strict standards must be held up, for mild religion is a mere night light futilely designed to ease the terrors of human existence. But real religion is a bright light that drives out the darkness, rather than simply pacifying us in the midst of darkness!

Of course, there are those Maginot-line Mormons who make the mistake of feeling unjustifiably secure, who are vulnerable on their flanks to the attacks of the world. There are also those who feel they can safely stay close to, but not in, the Church, but they will suffer the same fate as the red coal that is taken out of the bonfire and is left to itself.

Without, there are those who will chronically misunderstand the Church because they are so busy believing what they *want* to believe about the Church that they take no time to learn what they *need* to learn about the Church.

President Joseph F. Smith, who had considerable experience in such matters, warned us: "There are those who speak only evil of the Latter-day Saints. There are those––and they abound largely in our midst––who will shut their eyes to every virtue and to every good thing connected with this latter-day work, and will pour out floods of falsehood and misrepresentation against the people of God. I forgive them for this. I leave them in the hands of the just Judge." (*Gospel Doctrine,* p. 337.)

The same wise and forgiving prophet contrasted the courage "of men who are brave at heart" with "the courage of faith." The former breaks under some pressures, while the latter helps us when we have done all and "having done all, to stand." "Great causes," said President Smith, "are not won in a single generation." The "courage of faith" is, he said, "the courage of progress. Men who possess that divine quality go on." (Ibid., p. 119.)

If we think about it in any depth at all, surely we must realize that the most common pressure points in a dedicated disciple's life are bound to be how to give of one's time, talents, self, and means with proper priorities and righteous outcomes. The choices are seldom between holding a family home evening and robbing a bank! How can the test of our commitment and our judgment really be made without actually dealing with such choices as those involved in the wise use of time, talents, means—in sum, the management of self in the second estate? And is not sharpening our sense of timing also a part of maturing?

Tactical things often require a sense of timing. World War II cartoonist Bill Mauldin drew an American artillery spotter crouched in a foxhole over which a German tank was perched; the spotter said anxiously over the field telephone: "Able Fox Five to Able Fox, I got a target, but ya gotta be patient." (*Up Front* [Cleveland: World Publishing Co.], p. 10.)

Sometimes, as much as we would like to accelerate the chemistry in the Church, we must be patient; what is happening is not finished yet.

Almost all tests involve the interplay of time, talent, and means. These tests are most likely to produce self-pity when things don't go right. "I tried, didn't I?" "Why do I feel so miserable?" "Why do I feel so frustrated when I am trying to do what is right?" Consolation can come if we realize we are dealing with divine standards and mortal participants. The skills that can emerge can be learned only one way: like swimming, there is only so much to be taught at poolside, then one must get in the water!

If as we move along the path we can come to accept the reality that "death is only more life" (George Mac-Donald, *An Anthology,* p. 104), we will be freer men and women, less fearful and more filled with faith. We will be much better companions. We will also be able to say of some who violate the commandments of God and seem, nevertheless, to prosper, "So be it," for they have their reward––but in a perishable currency that is being devalued day by day.

We will also be able to ponder without flinching too much the paradox that arises when, for some, there is a sudden interruption of life and for others an unwanted prolongation of life. Sometimes we are ready when He is not, and other times He is ready when we are not. His readiness must be met by our willingness.

Meanwhile, with the gospel standards we can scrutinize the slogans and systems of man, accepting this, rejecting that. Knowing who men really are permits us, for instance, to examine what happens to the "you" in the latest political or economic utopia being proposed. We, more than others, should express effective concern for the "man" in management or the "brother" in various brotherhoods. We can be "wise as serpents, and harmless as doves" (Matthew 10:16) while doing such discerning things, using the unwavering standards of the gospel of Jesus Christ as our guide.

Possessed of, and feasting upon, these powerful truths, growing in our hope, in our love of God and man, and in our capacity to endure, we can "press forward" knowing that just ahead is Father. Inside that next and final gate there is perfect love and justice. We are also on the edge of even more enormous truths, deep truths that are best learned when Father can teach us personally.

The Japanese have a special word that means "restrained elegance." In many ways, the words of Christ are given to us with restrained elegance, because the scriptures are almost too rich for us even now. But this is simply an inviting intimation of what is yet to come. One cannot read and reread Nephi's words (the theme of this little volume) and fail to sense the restrained elegance in the imagery of the truths being conveyed by Nephi.

Having expended so many words describing the difficulties along the way, for they are real and relentless

130

enough, how then is one to attempt to explain the assurance from Jesus when He said, "For my yoke is easy, and my burden is light"? (Matthew 11:30.) There are some helps in understanding this seeming contradiction.

First, Jesus counseled, "Take my yoke upon you, *and learn of me;* for I am meek and lowly in heart: and ye shall find rest unto your souls." (Matthew 11:29. Italics added.) We cannot learn of him *unless* we assume his yoke. Just how things become not only bearable but easy—this immense insight we receive only *after* trying what Jesus urged.

Second, the Lord has actually eased the physical burdens placed upon his people, "that even you cannot feel them upon your backs." (Mosiah 24:14.) He did this by strengthening them; He made their burdens "light; yea, the Lord did strengthen them that they could bear up their burdens with ease, and they did submit cheerfully and with patience to all the will of the Lord." (Mosiah 24:15.) The kilograms were constant but the bearer's capacity was increased. The same is done with regard to other kinds of burdens.

Third, among the covenants of citizenship in the kingdom is a willingness "to bear one another's burdens, that they may be light." (Mosiah 18:8.) We have a responsibility to lighten each other's load.

Fourth, Alma tells us that the sprouting and swelling of the gospel seed (Alma 32 and 33) must be followed by its nourishment by faith so that it will grow and "become a tree, springing up . . . unto everlasting life." Then, he says, God will "grant unto you that your burdens may be light, through the joy of his Son. And even all this can ye do if ye will. Amen." (Alma 33:23.)

Jesus' promise is so profound but some things seem clear:

1. It is no use contemplating, measuring, and studying one's cross; it must be picked up! Studying it from a distance is not the same as shouldering it.

2. Further, a cross is best carried when we keep mov-

ing, for once put down, it is heavier than ever to reshoulder.

3. We are not loaded with burdens beyond our capacity. We could never carry His cross, but we can carry ours, and we will learn about Him by so doing, and by doing so meekly, cheerfully, and with patience. It is not easy at first, for we could not appreciate Him if there were immediate ease.

4. By bearing the burdens placed upon us, we, as saints should, can have a portion of "his joy," which will also lighten the load.

5. Finally, we must do as this book's theme-giver, Nephi, said--". . . go and do the things which the Lord hath commanded," knowing that the Lord gives us no tasks except He prepares the way for us to "accomplish the thing which he commandeth." (1 Nephi 3:7.)

The Lord does not divulge in advance how we will ever make it, carrying our little crosses through trials, tribulations, and just plain old everyday growing experiences. But the way is prepared, the variables have been divinely computed, talents and tasks have been matched, and the interpersonal challenges correlated. These things we need not know the details of now. For us, it remains to "go and do"! Yes, to shoulder the burdens and to "press forward."

Awaiting the faithful is God's greatest gift of all-- eternal life (D&C 14:7)--for which all humans will have had an equal chance to strive. The gift of immortality to all is so choice a gift that our rejoicing in these two great and generous gifts should drown out any sorrow, assuage any grief, conquer any mood, dissolve any despair, and tame any tragedy.

Even those who see life as pointless will one day point with adoration to the performance of the Man of Galilee in the crowded moments of time known as Gethsemane and Calvary. Those who now say life is meaningless will yet applaud the atonement, which saved us all from meaninglessness.

Christ's victory over death routs the rationale that

there is a general and irreversible human predicament; there are only personal predicaments, but even from these we can also be rescued by following the pathway of Him who rescued us from general extinction.

A disciple's "brightness of hope," therefore, means that at funerals his tears are not because of termination, but because of interruption and separation. Though just as wet, his tears are not of despair, but of appreciation and anticipation. Yes, for disciples, the closing of a grave is but the closing of a door that will later be flung open.

It is the Garden Tomb, not life, that is empty!

INDEX

136